9/06

GHOST STORIES

Haunted

GARETH**STEVENS**

PUBLISHING

A Member of the WRC Media Family of Companies

Please visit our web site at: www.garethstevens.com
For a free color catalog describing Gareth Stevens Publishing's
list of high-quality books and multimedia programs, call
1-800-542-2595 (USA) or 1-800-387-3178 (Canada).
Gareth Stevens Publishing's fax: (414) 332-3567.

Library of Congress Cataloging-in-Publication Data

Haunted.
       v. cm. — (Ghost stories)
    ISBN-10: 0-8368-6824-2 — ISBN-13: 978-0-8368-6824-1 (lib. bdg.)
    1. Children's stories.   2. Ghost stories.   [1. Short stories.
    2. Ghosts—Fiction.]   I. Series.
    PZ5.H28   2006
    [Fic]—dc22   2006012804

This North American edition first published in 2007 by
Gareth Stevens Publishing
A Member of the WRC Media Family of Companies
330 West Olive Street, Suite 100
Milwaukee, WI 53212 USA

This U.S. edition copyright © 2007 by Gareth Stevens, Inc.
Original edition copyright © 2005 by Miles Kelly Publishing Ltd.
First published in Great Britain in 2005 by Bardfield Press,
Bardfield Centre, Great Bardfield, Essex, CM7 4SL, United Kingdom.

Series editorial director: Belinda Gallagher
Series art director: Jo Brewer
Series assistant editors: Rosalind McGuire and Hannah Todd
Series designer: Tom Slemmings
Series picture research manager: Liberty Newton
Series picture researcher: Laura Faulder
Series production: Estela Boulton and Elizabeth Brunwin
Series scanning and reprographics: Anthony Cambray, Mike Coupe, and Ian Paulyn
Introduction ("Haunted"): Vic Parker

Gareth Stevens editorial direction: Mark J. Sachner
Gareth Stevens editor: Tea Benduhn
Gareth Stevens art direction and design: Tammy West
Gareth Stevens art design: Scott Krall and Kami Strunsee
Gareth Stevens production: Jessica Morris and Robert Kraus

Artwork and photographic credits: Martin Angel, Vanessa Card, Castrol, CMCD, CORBIS,
Corel digitalSTOCK, Jon Davis/Linden Artists, Peter Dennis/Linda Rogers Associates, digitalvision,
Flat Earth, John Foxx, Hemera, Richard Hook/Linden Artists, ILN, PhotoAlto, PhotoDisc, PhotoEssentials,
PhotoPro, Eric Rowe/Linden Artists, Mike Saunders, StockbyteColin Sullivan/Beehive Illustration,
Gwen Tourret/B. L. Kearley, Rudi Vizi, Mike White/Temple Rogers. All other artworks are from
the Miles Kelly Artwork Bank.

Printed in the United States of America

1 2 3 4 5 6 7 8 9 10 09 08 07 06

TABLE OF CONTENTS

Haunted

WHETHER FAR OR NEAR, ON LAND OR AT SEA, LONG AGO

OR RIGHT NOW, GHOSTS AND GHOULS HAUNT ONLY AN UNFORTUNATE

FEW. THIS, OF COURSE, IS LUCKY FOR MOST,

BUT EXTREMELY UNLUCKY FOR SOME.

Haunted is filled with creepy stories to chill you, thrill you, and send shivers down your spine. Here are some of the very best from a rich tradition of terrifying tales that dates back to Christmas Eve, 1764. It was then that the first ever "horror" novel was published, *The Castle of Otranto*, by Horace Walpole. His was an eerie tale of ghosts, family curses, and macabre goings-on, set in a foreign land during medieval times – an era when everyone believed in the supernatural and many superstitions made them fearful. *The Castle of Otranto* captivated the imagination of eighteenth-century readers who demanded more eerie tales.

Through the Victorian era (1837–1901), families and friends loved to gather around the parlor fire on dark evenings to listen to sinister and spooky stories. Spiritualism also became fashionable, and many Victorians dabbled in attempts to contact the dead. Victorian authors transformed Gothic horror-writing by developing it in exciting directions. They did away with remote locations and past times and brought horrors to their readers' front doors.

In 1918, Virginia Woolf wrote an article for the *Times Literary Supplement* exploring the reasons that ghost stories are so irresistible. She decided that "It is pleasant to be afraid when we are conscious that we are in no kind of danger."

So settle back and enjoy these haunting tales, safe in the knowledge that there's no such thing as a ghost... or is there?

THE CANTERVILLE GHOST

Oscar Wilde

Extract

As Canterville Chase is seven miles from Ascot, the nearest railway station, Mr. Otis had telegraphed for a wagonette to meet them, and they started on their drive in high spirits. It was a lovely July evening, and the air was delicate with the scent of the pine woods. Now and then they heard a wood pigeon brooding over its own sweet voice, or saw, deep in the rustling fern, the burnished breast of the pheasant. Little squirrels peered at them from the beech trees as they went by, and the rabbits scudded away through the brushwood and over the mossy knolls, with their white tails in the air. As they entered the avenue of Canterville Chase, however, the sky became suddenly overcast with clouds, a curious stillness seemed to hold the atmosphere, a great flight of rooks passed silently over their heads, and, before they reached the house, some big drops of rain had fallen.

Standing on the steps to receive them was an old woman, neatly dressed in black silk, with a white cap and apron. This was Mrs. Umney, the housekeeper, whom Mrs. Otis, at Lady Canterville's earnest request, had consented to keep on in her former position. She made them each a low curtsy as they alighted, and said in a quaint, old-fashioned manner, "I bid you welcome to Canterville Chase." Following her, they passed through the fine Tudor hall into the library, a long, low room, paneled in black oak, at the end of which was a large stained-glass window. Here they found tea laid out for them, and, after taking off their wraps, they sat down and began to look round, while Mrs. Umney waited on them.

Suddenly Mrs. Otis caught sight of a dull red stain on the floor just by the fireplace and, quite unconscious of what it really signified, said to Mrs. Umney, "I am afraid something has been spilled there."

"Yes, madam," replied the old housekeeper in a low voice, "blood has been spilt on that spot."

"How horrid," cried Mrs. Otis. "I don't at all care for bloodstains in a sitting room. It must be removed at once."

The old woman smiled, and answered in the same low, mysterious voice, "It is the blood of Lady Eleanore de Canterville, who was murdered on that very spot by her own husband, Sir Simon de Canterville, in 1575. Sir Simon survived her nine years, and disappeared suddenly under very mysterious circumstances. His body has never been discovered, but his guilty spirit still haunts the Chase. The bloodstain has been much admired by tourists and others, and cannot be removed."

"That is all nonsense," cried Washington Otis. "Pinkerton's Champion Stain Remover and Paragon Detergent will clean it up in no time," and before the terrified housekeeper could interfere, he had fallen upon his knees and was scouring the floor with a small stick of what looked like a black cosmetic. In a few moments no trace of the bloodstain could be seen.

"I knew Pinkerton would do it," he exclaimed triumphantly, as he looked round at his admiring family; but no sooner had he said these words than a terrible flash of lightning lit up the somber room, a fearful peal of thunder made them all start to their feet, and Mrs. Umney fainted.

"What a monstrous climate!" said the American Minister calmly, as he lit a long cheroot. "I guess the old country is so overpopulated that they have not enough decent weather for everybody. I have always been of opinion that emigration is the only thing for England."

"My dear Hiram," cried Mrs. Otis, "what can we do with a woman who faints?"

"Charge it to her like breakages," answered the Minister, "she won't faint after that." And in a few moments Mrs. Umney certainly came to. There was no doubt, however, that she was extremely upset, and she sternly warned Mr. Otis to beware of some trouble coming to the house.

"I have seen things with my own eyes, sir," she said, "that would make any Christian's hair stand on end, and many and many a night I have not closed my eyes in sleep for the awful things that are done here." Mr. Otis, however, and his wife warmly assured the honest soul that they were not afraid of ghosts, and, after invoking the blessings of Providence on her new master and mistress, and making arrangements for an increase of salary, the old housekeeper tottered off to her room.

The storm raged fiercely all that night, but nothing of particular note occurred. The next morning, however, when they came down to breakfast, they found the terrible stain of blood once again on the floor. "I don't think it can be the fault of the Paragon Detergent," said Washington, "for I have tried it with everything. It must be the ghost." He accordingly rubbed out the stain a second time, but the second morning it appeared again. The third morning also it was there, though the library had been locked up at night by Mr. Otis himself, and the key carried upstairs. The whole family were now quite interested; Mr. Otis began to suspect that he had been too dogmatic in his denial of the existence of ghosts, Mrs. Otis expressed her intention of joining the Psychical Society, and Washington prepared a long letter to Messrs. Myers and Podmore on the subject of the permanence of sanguineous stains when connected with crime. That night all doubts about the objective existence of phantasmata were removed forever.

The day had been warm and sunny; and, in the cool of the evening, the whole family went out for a drive. They did not return home till nine o'clock, when they had a light supper. The conversation in no way turned upon ghosts, so there were not even those primary conditions of receptive expectation which so often precede the presentation of psychical phenomena. The subjects discussed, as I have since learned from Mr. Otis, were merely such as form the ordinary conversation of cultured Americans of the better class, such as the immense superiority of Miss Fanny Davenport over Sarah Bernhardt as an actress; the difficulty of obtaining green corn, buckwheat cakes, and hominy, even in the best English houses; the importance of Boston in the development of the world-soul; the advantages of the baggage check system in railway traveling; and the sweetness of the New York accent as compared to the London drawl. No mention at all was made of the supernatural, nor was Sir Simon de Canterville alluded to in any way. At eleven o'clock the family retired and by half-past all the lights were out. Some time after, Mr. Otis was awakened by a curious noise in the corridor, outside his room. It sounded like the clank of metal, and seemed to be coming nearer every moment. He got up at once, struck a match, and looked at the time. It was exactly one o'clock. He was quite calm, and felt his pulse, which was not at all feverish. The strange noise still continued, and with it he heard distinctly the sound of footsteps. He put on his slippers, took a small oblong phial out of his dressing-case, and opened the door. Right in front of him he saw, in the wan moonlight, an old man of terrible aspect. His eyes were as red as burning coals; long gray hair fell over his shoulders in matted coils; his garments, which were of antique cut, were soiled and ragged; and from his wrists and ankles hung heavy manacles and rusty shackles.

"My dear sir," said Mr. Otis, "I really must insist on your oiling those chains, and have brought you for that purpose a small bottle of the Tammany Rising Sun Lubricator. It is said to be completely efficacious upon one application, and there are several testimonials to that effect on the wrapper from some of our most eminent native divines. I shall leave it here for you by the bedroom candles, and will be happy to supply you with more should you require it." With these words the United States Minister laid the bottle down on a marble table, and, closing his door, retired to rest.

For a moment the Canterville ghost stood quite motionless in natural indignation; then, dashing the bottle violently upon the polished floor, he fled down the corridor, uttering hollow groans, and emitting a ghastly green light. Just, however, as he reached the top of the great oak staircase, a door was flung open, two little white-robed figures appeared, and a large pillow whizzed past his head! There was evidently no time to be lost, so, hastily adopting the fourth dimension of space as a means of escape, he vanished through the wainscoting, and the house became quite quiet.

On reaching a small secret chamber in the left wing, he leaned up against a moonbeam to recover his breath, and began to try and realize his position. Never, in a brilliant and uninterrupted career of three hundred years, had he been so grossly insulted. He thought of the Dowager Duchess, whom he had frightened into a fit as she stood before the glass in her lace and diamonds; of the four housemaids, who had gone off into hysterics when he merely grinned at them through the curtains of one of the spare bedrooms; of the rector of the parish, whose candle he had blown out as he was coming late one night from the library, and who had been under the care of Sir William Gull ever since, a perfect martyr to nervous disorders; and of old Madame de Tremouillac, who, having wakened up one morning early and seen a skeleton seated in an armchair by the fire reading her diary, had been confined to her bed for six weeks with an attack of brain fever, and, on her recovery, had become reconciled to the Church, and had broken off her connection with that notorious sceptic Monsieur de Voltaire. He remembered the terrible night when the wicked Lord Canterville was found choking in his dressing room, with the knave of diamonds half way down his throat, and confessed, just before he died, that he had cheated Charles James Fox out of £50,000 at Crockford's by means of that very card, and swore that the ghost had made him swallow it. All his great achievements came back to him again, from the butler who had shot himself in the pantry because he had seen a green hand tapping at the window pane, to the beautiful Lady Stutfield, who was always obliged to wear a black velvet band round her throat to hide the mark of five fingers burnt upon her white skin, and who drowned herself at last in the carp-pond at the end of the King's Walk. With the enthusiastic egotism of the true artist he went over his most celebrated performances, and smiled bitterly to himself as he recalled to mind his last appearance as "Red Ruben, or the Strangled Babe," his debut as "Gaunt Gibeon, the Blood-sucker of Bexley Moor," and the furore he had excited one lovely June evening by merely playing ninepins with his own bones upon the lawn-tennis ground. And after all this, some wretched modern Americans were to come and offer him the Rising Sun Lubricator, and throw pillows at his head! It was unbearable. Besides, no ghosts in history had ever been treated in this manner. Accordingly, he determined to have vengeance, and remained till daylight in deep thought.

The next morning when the Otis family met at breakfast, they discussed the ghost at some length. The United States Minister was naturally a little annoyed to find that his present had not been accepted. "I have no wish," he said, "to do the ghost any personal injury, and I must say that, considering the length of time he has been in the house, I don't think it is at all polite to throw pillows at him" – a very just remark, at which, I am sorry to say, the twins burst into shouts of laughter. "Upon the other hand," he continued, "if he really declines to use the Rising Sun Lubricator, we shall have to take his chains from him. It would be quite impossible to sleep with such a noise going on outside the bedrooms."

For the rest of the week, however, they were undisturbed; the only thing that excited any attention being the continual renewal of the bloodstain on the library floor. This certainly was very strange, as the door was always locked at night by Mr. Otis, and the windows kept closely barred. The chameleon-like color, also, of the stain excited a good deal of comment. Some mornings it was a dull red, then it would be vermilion, then a rich purple, and once when they came down for family prayers, according to the simple rites of the Free American Reformed Episcopalian Church, they found it a bright emerald green. These kaleidoscopic changes naturally amused the party very much, and bets on the subject were freely made every evening. The only person who did not enter into the joke was little Virginia, who, for some unexplained reason, was always a good deal distressed at the sight of the bloodstain, and very nearly cried the morning it was emerald green.

The second appearance of the ghost was on Sunday night. Shortly after they had gone to bed they were suddenly alarmed by a fearful crash in the hall. Rushing downstairs, they found that a large suit of old armor had become detached from its stand, and had fallen on the stone floor, while, seated in a high-backed chair, was the Canterville ghost, rubbing his knees with an expression of acute agony on his face. The twins, having brought their peashooters with them, at once discharged two pellets on him, with that accuracy of aim which can only be attained by long and careful practice on a writing-master, while the United States Minister covered him with his revolver, and called upon him, in accordance with Californian etiquette, to hold up his hands! The ghost started up with a wild shriek of rage, and swept through them like a mist, extinguishing Washington Otis's candle as he passed, and so leaving them all in total darkness. On reaching the top of the staircase he recovered himself and determined to give his celebrated peal of demonic laughter. This he had on more than one occasion found extremely useful. It was said to have turned Lord Raker's wig gray in a single night, and had certainly made three of Lady Canterville's French governesses give warning before their month was up. He accordingly laughed his most horrible laugh, till the old vaulted roof rang and rang again, but hardly had the fearful echo died away when a door opened, and Mrs. Otis came out in a light blue dressing gown.

"I am afraid you are far from well," she said, "and have brought you a bottle of Dr. Dobell's Tincture. If it is indigestion, you will find it a most excellent remedy." The ghost glared at her in fury, and began at once to make preparations for turning himself into a large black dog, an accomplishment for which he was justly renowned, and to which the family doctor always attributed the permanent idiocy of Lord Canterville's uncle, the Hon. Thomas Horton. The sound of approaching footsteps, however, made him hesitate in his fell purpose, so he contented himself with becoming faintly phosphorescent, and vanished with a deep churchyard groan, just as the twins had come up to him.

On reaching his room he entirely broke down, and became a prey to the most violent agitation. The vulgarity of the twins, and the gross materialism of Mrs. Otis, were naturally extremely annoying, but what really distressed him most was that he had been unable to wear the suit of mail. He had hoped that even modern Americans would be thrilled by the sight of a Specter In Armor, if for no more sensible reason, at least out of respect for their national poet Longfellow, over whose graceful and attractive poetry he himself had whiled away many a weary hour when the Cantervilles were up in town. Besides, it was his own suit. He had worn it with success at the Kenilworth tournament, and had been highly complimented on it by no less a person than the Virgin Queen herself. Yet when he had put it on, he had been completely overpowered by the weight of the huge breastplate and steel casque, and had fallen heavily on the stone pavement, barking both his knees severely and bruising the knuckles of his right hand.

For some days after this he was extremely ill, and hardly stirred out of his room at all, except to keep the blood stain in proper repair. However, by taking great care of himself he recovered, and resolved to make a third attempt to frighten the United States Minister and his family. He a selected Friday the 17th of August for his appearance, and spent most of that day in looking over his wardrobe, ultimately deciding in favor of a large slouched hat with a red feather, a winding-sheet frilled at the wrists and neck, and a rusty sword. Toward evening a violent storm of rain came on, and the wind was so high that all the windows and doors in the old house shook and rattled. In fact, it was just such weather as he loved. His plan of action was this: He was to make his way quietly to Washington Otis's room, gibber at him from the foot of the bed, and stab himself three times in the throat to the sound of slow music. He bore Washington a special grudge, being quite aware that it was he who was in the habit of removing the famous Canterville blood stain, by means of Pinkerton's Paragon Detergent. Having reduced the reckless and foolhardy youth to a condition of abject terror, he was then to proceed to the room occupied by the United States Minister and his wife, and there to place a clammy hand on Mrs. Otis's forehead, while he hissed into her trembling husband's ear the awful secrets of the charnel house. With regard to little Virginia, he had not quite made up his mind. She had never insulted him in any way, and was pretty and gentle. A few hollow groans from the wardrobe, he thought, would be more than sufficient, or, if that failed to wake her, he might grabble at the counterpane with palsy-twitching fingers. As for the twins, he was quite determined to teach them a lesson. The first thing to be done was, of course, to sit upon their chests, so as to produce the stifling sensation of nightmare. Then, as their beds were quite close to each other, to stand between them in the form of a green, icy-cold corpse, till they became paralyzed with fear. And finally, to throw off the winding-sheet and crawl round the room, with white bleached bones and one rolling eyeball, in the character of "Dumb Daniel, or the Suicide's Skeleton," a role in which he had on more than one occasion produced a great effect, and which he considered quite equal to his famous part of "Martin the Maniac, or the Masked Mystery."

At half past ten he heard the family going to bed. For some time he was disturbed by wild shrieks of laughter from the twins, who, with the lighthearted gaiety of schoolboys, were evidently amusing themselves before they retired to rest, but at a quarter past eleven all was still, and, as midnight sounded, he sallied forth. The owl beat against the window panes, the raven croaked from the old yew tree, and the wind wandered moaning round the house like a lost soul; but the Otis family slept unconscious of their doom, and high above the rain and storm he could hear the steady snoring of the

Minister for the United States. He stepped stealthily out of the wainscoting, with an evil smile on his cruel, wrinkled mouth, and the moon hid her face in a cloud as he stole past the great oriel window, where his own arms and those of his murdered wife were blazoned in azure and gold. On and on he glided, like an evil shadow, the very darkness seeming to loathe him as he passed. Once he thought he heard something call, and stopped; but it was only the baying of a dog from the Red Farm, and he went on, muttering strange sixteenth-century curses, and ever and anon brandishing the rusty sword in the midnight air. Finally he reached the corner of the passage that led to luckless Washington's room. For a moment he paused there, the wind blowing his long gray locks about his head, and twisting into grotesque and fantastic folds the nameless horror of the dead man's shroud. Then the clock struck the quarter, and he felt the time was come. He chuckled to himself and turned the corner; but no sooner had he done so, than, with a piteous wail of terror, he fell back, and hid his blanched face in his long, bony hands. Right in front of him was standing a horrible specter, motionless as a carven image, and monstrous as a madman's dream! Its head was bald and burnished; its face round, and fat, and white; and hideous laughter seemed to have writhed its features into an eternal grin. From the eyes streamed rays of scarlet light, the mouth was a wide well of fire, and a hideous garment, like to his own, swathed with its silent snows the Titan form. On its breast was a placard with strange writing in antique characters – some scroll of shame it seemed, some record of wild sins, some awful calendar of crime – and, with its right hand, it bore aloft a fashion of gleaming steel.

Never having seen a ghost before, he naturally was terribly frightened and, after a second hasty glance at the awful phantom, he fled back to his room, tripping up in his long winding-sheet as he sped down the corridor, and finally dropping the rusty sword into the Minister's jack boots, where it was found in the morning by the butler. Once in the privacy of his own apartment, he flung himself down on a small pallet-bed and hid his face under the clothes. After a time, however, the brave old Canterville spirit asserted itself and he determined to go and speak to the other ghost as soon as it was daylight. Accordingly, just as the dawn was touching the hills with silver, he returned toward the spot where he had first laid eyes on the grisly phantom, feeling that, after all, two ghosts were better than one, and that, by the aid of his new friend, he might safely grapple with the twins. On reaching the spot, however, a terrible sight met his gaze. Something had evidently happened to the specter, for the light had entirely faded from its hollow eyes, the gleaming sword had fallen from its hand, and it was leaning up against the wall in a strained and uncomfortable attitude. He rushed forward and seized it in his arms, when, to his horror, the head slipped off and rolled on the floor, the body assumed a recumbent posture, and he found himself clasping a white dimity bed-curtain, with a sweeping brush, a kitchen cleaver, and a hollow turnip lying at his feet! Unable to understand this curious transformation, he clutched the placard with feverish haste, and there, in the gray morning light, he read these fearful words:

YE OTIS GHOSTE

YE ONLIE TRUE AND ORIGINALE SPOOK
BEWARE OF YE IMITATIONES
ALL OTHERS ARE COUNTERFEITE

The whole thing flashed across him. He had been tricked, foiled, and outwitted! The old Canterville look came into his eyes; he ground his toothless gums together; and, raising his withered hands high above his head, swore, according to the picturesque phraseology of the antique school, that when Chanticleer had sounded twice his merry horn, deeds of blood would be wrought, and Murder walk abroad with silent feet.

Hardly had he finished this awful oath when, from the red-tiled roof of a distant homestead, a cock crowew. He laughed a long, low, bitter laugh, and waited. Hour after hour he waited, but the cock, for some strange reason, did not crow again. Finally, at half past seven, the arrival of the housemaids made him give up his fearful vigil, and

he stalked back to his room, thinking of his vain hope
and baffled purpose. There he consulted several books
of ancient chivalry, of which he was exceedingly fond,
and found that, on every occasion on which his oath had
been used, Chanticleer had always crowed a second time.
"Perdition seize the naughty fowl," he muttered, "I have
seen the day when, with my stout spear, I would have run
him through the gorge, and made him crow for me as 'twere
in death!" He then retired to a comfortable lead coffin, and
stayed there till evening.

The next day the ghost was very weak and tired. The terrible
excitement of the last four weeks was beginning to have its
effect. His nerves were completely shattered, and he started
at the slightest noise. For five days he kept to his room,
and at last made up his mind to give up the point of the
bloodstain on the library floor. If the Otis family did not want
it, they clearly did not deserve it. They were evidently people
on a low, material plane of existence, and quite incapable
of appreciating the symbolic value of sensuous phenomena.
The question of phantasmic apparitions and the development
of astral bodies, was of course quite a different matter, and
really not under his control. It was his solemn duty to appear
in the corridor once a week, and to gibber from the large oriel
window on the first and third Wednesday in every month,
and he did not see how he could honorably escape from his
obligations. It is quite true that his life had been very evil,
but, upon the other hand, he was most conscientious in all

things connected with the supernatural. For the next three Saturdays, accordingly, he traversed the corridor as usual between midnight and three o'clock, taking every possible precaution against being either heard or seen. He removed his boots, trod as lightly as possible on the old worm-eaten boards, wore a large black velvet cloak, and was careful to use the Rising Sun Lubricator for oiling his chains. I am bound to acknowledge that it was with a good deal of difficulty that he brought himself to adopt this last mode of protection. However, one night, while the family were at dinner, he slipped into Mr. Otis's bedroom and carried off the bottle. He felt a little humiliated at first, but afterward was sensible enough to see that there was a great deal to be said for the invention, and, to a certain degree, it served his purpose. Still, in spite of everything, he was not left unmolested. Strings were continually being stretched across the corridor, over which he tripped in the dark, and on one occasion, while dressed for the part of "Black Isaac, or the Huntsman of Hogley Woods," he met with a severe fall through treading on a butter-slide, which the twins had constructed from the entrance of the Tapestry Chamber to the top of the oak staircase. This last insult so enraged him that he resolved to make one final effort to assert his dignity and social position and determined to visit the insolent young Etonians the next night in his celebrated character of "Reckless Rupert, or the Headless Earl."

He had not appeared in this disguise for more than seventy years; in fact, not since he had so frightened pretty Lady

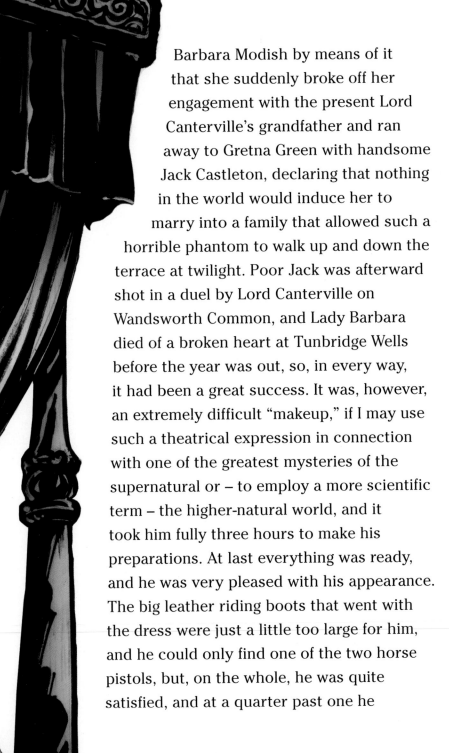

Barbara Modish by means of it that she suddenly broke off her engagement with the present Lord Canterville's grandfather and ran away to Gretna Green with handsome Jack Castleton, declaring that nothing in the world would induce her to marry into a family that allowed such a horrible phantom to walk up and down the terrace at twilight. Poor Jack was afterward shot in a duel by Lord Canterville on Wandsworth Common, and Lady Barbara died of a broken heart at Tunbridge Wells before the year was out, so, in every way, it had been a great success. It was, however, an extremely difficult "makeup," if I may use such a theatrical expression in connection with one of the greatest mysteries of the supernatural or – to employ a more scientific term – the higher-natural world, and it took him fully three hours to make his preparations. At last everything was ready, and he was very pleased with his appearance. The big leather riding boots that went with the dress were just a little too large for him, and he could only find one of the two horse pistols, but, on the whole, he was quite satisfied, and at a quarter past one he

24

glided out of the wainscoting and crept down the corridor. On reaching the room occupied by the twins, which I should mention was called the Blue Bed Chamber, on account of the color of its hangings, he found the door just ajar. Wishing to make an effective entrance, he flung it wide open, when a heavy jug of water fell right down on him, wetting him to the skin, and just missing his left shoulder by a couple of inches. At the same moment he heard stifled shrieks of laughter proceeding from the four-poster bed. The shock to his nervous system was so great that he fled back to his room as hard as he could go, and the next day he was laid up with a severe cold. The only thing that at all consoled him in the whole affair was the fact that he had not brought his head with him, for, had he done so, the consequences might have been very serious.

He now gave up all hope of ever frightening this rude, noisy American family, and contented himself as a general rule, with creeping about the passages in list slippers, with a thick red muffler round his throat for fear of drafts, and a small gun, in case he should be attacked by the dreaded twins. The final blow he received occurred on the 19th of September. He had gone downstairs to the great entrance hall, feeling sure that there, at any rate, he would be quite unmolested, and was amusing himself by making satiric remarks on the large Saroni photographs of the United States Minister and his wife, which had now taken the place of the Canterville family pictures. He was simply but neatly clad in a long shroud, spotted with churchyard mold, and had tied up his jaw with a strip of yellow linen. He carried a small lantern and a sexton's spade. In fact, he was dressed for the character of "Jonas the Graveless, or the Corpse-Snatcher of Chertsey Barn," one of his most remarkable impersonations, and one which the Cantervilles had every reason to remember, as it was the real origin of their quarrel with their neighbor, Lord Rufford. It was about a quarter past two o'clock in the morning, and, as far as he could ascertain, no one was stirring. As he was strolling towards the library, however, to see if there were any traces left of the blood stain, suddenly there leaped out on him from a dark corner two figures, who waved their arms wildly above their heads, and shrieked "BOO!" in his ear.

Seized with a panic, which, under the circumstances, was only natural, he rushed for the staircase, but found Washington Otis waiting for him there with the big garden syringe; and being thus hemmed in by his enemies on every side, and driven almost to bay, he vanished into the great iron stove, which, fortunately for him, was not lit, and had to make his way home through the flues and chimneys, arriving at his own room in a terrible state of dirt, disorder, and despair.

After this he was not seen again on any nocturnal expedition. The twins lay in wait for him on several occasions, and strewed the passages with nutshells every night to the great annoyance of their parents and the servants, but it was of no avail. It was quite evident that his feelings were so wounded that he would not appear. Mr. Otis consequently resumed his great work on the history of the Democratic Party, on which he had been engaged for some years; Mrs. Otis organized a wonderful clambake, which amazed the whole county; the boys took to lacrosse, euchre, poker, and other American national games; and Virginia rode about the lanes on her pony, accompanied by the young Duke of Cheshire, who had come to spend the last week of his holidays at Canterville Chase. It was generally assumed that the ghost had gone away, and, in fact, Mr. Otis wrote a letter to that effect to Lord Canterville, who, in reply, expressed his great pleasure at the news, and sent his best congratulations to the Minister's wife.

The Otises, however, were deceived, for the ghost was still in the house, and though now almost an invalid, was by no means ready to let matters

rest, particularly as he heard that among the guests was the young Duke of Cheshire, whose grand-uncle, Lord Francis Stilton, had once bet a hundred guineas with Colonel Carbury that he would play dice with the Canterville ghost, and was found the next morning lying on the floor of the card room in such a helpless paralytic state, that though he lived on to a great age, he was never able to say anything again but "Double Sixes." The story was well known at the time, though, of course, out of respect to the feelings of the two noble families, every attempt was made to hush it up; and a full account of all the circumstances connected with it will be found in the third volume of Lord Tattle's Recollections of the Prince Regent and His Friends. The ghost, then, was naturally very anxious to show that he had not lost his influence over the Stiltons, with whom indeed, he was distantly connected, his own first cousin having been married en secondes noces to the Sieur de Bulkeley, from whom, as everyone knows, the Dukes of Cheshire are lineally descended. Accordingly, he made arrangements for appearing to Virginia's little lover in his celebrated impersonation of "The Vampire Monk, or, the Bloodless Benedictine," a performance so horrible that when old Lady Startup saw it, which she did on one fatal New Year's

Eve, in the year 1764, she went off into the most piercing shrieks, which culminated in violent apoplexy, and died in three days, after disinheriting the Cantervilles, who were her nearest relations, and leaving all her money to her London apothecary. At the last moment, however, his terror of the twins prevented his leaving his room, and the little Duke slept in peace under the great feathered canopy in the Royal Bedchamber, and dreamed of Virginia.

THE NARRATIVE OF THE GHOST OF A HAND

J. Sheridan Le Fanu

I 'm sure she believed every word she related, for old Sally
was veracious. But all this was worth just so much as
such talk commonly is – marvels, fabulae, what our
ancestors called winter's tales – which gathered details from
every narrator and dilated in the act of narration. Still it was
not quite for nothing that the house was held to be haunted.
Under all this smoke there smoldered just a little spark of
truth – an authenticated mystery, for the solution of which
some of my readers may possibly suggest a theory, though
I confess I can't.

Miss Rebecca Chattesworth, in a letter dated late in the
autumn of 1753, gives a minute and curious relation of

occurrences in the Tiled House, which, it is plain – although at starting she protests against all such fooleries – she has heard with a peculiar sort of interest and relates it certainly with an awful sort of particularity.

I was for printing the entire letter, which is really very singular as well as characteristic. But my publisher meets me with his veto; and I believe he is right. The worthy old lady's letter is, perhaps, too long; and I must rest content with a few hungry notes of its tenor.

That year, and somewhere about the 24th October, there broke out a strange dispute between Mr. Alderman Harper, of High Street, Dublin, and my Lord Castlemallard, who, in virtue of his cousinship to the young heir's mother, had undertaken for him the management of the tiny estate on which the Tiled or Tyled House – for I find it spelled both ways – stood.

This Alderman Harper had agreed for a lease of the house for his daughter, who was married to a gentleman named Prosser. He furnished it and put up hangings and otherwise went to considerable expense. Mr. and Mrs. Prosser came there sometime in June, and after having parted with a good many servants in the interval, she made up her mind that she could not live in the house; and her father waited on Lord Castlemallard and told him plainly that he would not take out the lease because the house was subjected to annoyances which he could not explain. In plain terms, he said it was haunted and that no servants would live there more than a few weeks and that after what his son-in-law's family had suffered there, not only should he be excused from taking a

lease of it, but that the house itself ought to be pulled down as a nuisance and the habitual haunt of something worse than human malefactors.

Lord Castlemallard filed a bill in the Equity side of the Exchequer to compel Mr. Alderman Harper to perform his contract, by taking out the lease. But the Alderman drew an answer, supported by no less than seven long affidavits, copies of all which were furnished to his lordship, and with the desired effect; for rather than compel him to place them upon the file of the court, his lordship struck, and consented to release him. I am sorry the cause did not proceed at least far enough to place upon the files of the court the very authentic and unaccountable story which Miss Rebecca relates.

The annoyances described did not begin till the end of August. One evening, Mrs. Prosser, quite alone, was sitting in the twilight at the back parlor window. It was open, and looking out into the orchard she plainly saw a hand stealthily placed upon the stone window sill outside, as if by someone beneath the window at her right side, intending to climb up. There was nothing but the hand, which was rather short but handsomely formed and white and plump, laid on the edge of the window sill; and it was not a very young hand, but one aged somewhere about forty, as she conjectured. It was only a few weeks before that the horrible robbery at Clondalkin had taken place and the lady fancied that the hand was that of one of the miscreants who was now about to scale the windows of

33

the Tiled House. She uttered a loud scream and an exclamation of terror and at the same moment the hand was quietly withdrawn.

Search was made in the orchard, but no indications of any person's having been under the window, beneath which, ranged along the wall, stood a great column of flower pots, which it seemed must have prevented anyone's coming within reach of it.

The same night there came a hasty tapping every now and then at the window of the kitchen. The women grew frightened and the servant-man, taking firearms with him, opened the back door, but discovered nothing. As he shut it, however, he said, "A thump came on it," and a pressure as of somebody striving to force his way in, which frightened him; and though the tapping went on upon the kitchen window panes, he made no further explorations.

About six o'clock on the Saturday evening following, the cook, "an honest, sober woman, now aged nigh sixty years," being alone in the kitchen, saw on looking up, it is supposed, the same fat but aristocratic-looking hand, laid with its palm against the glass, near the side of the window and this time moving slowly up and down, pressed all the while against the glass as if feeling carefully for some inequality in its surface. She cried out and said something like a prayer on seeing it. But it was not withdrawn for several seconds after.

After this, for a great many nights, there came at first a low and afterward an angry rapping, as it seemed with a set of clenched knuckles, at the back door. And the servant-man would not open it, but called to know who was there; and there came no answer, only a sound as if the palm of the hand was placed against it, and drawn slowly from side to side with a sort of soft, groping motion.

All this time, sitting in the back parlor, which for the time they used as a drawing room, Mr. and Mrs. Prosser were disturbed by rappings at the window, sometimes very low and furtive, like a clandestine signal, and at others sudden and so loud as to threaten the breaking of the pane.

This was all at the back of the house, which looked upon the orchard as you know. But on a Tuesday night, at about half past nine, there came precisely the same rapping at the hall door; and it went on, to the great annoyance of the master and terror of his wife, at intervals, for nearly two hours.

After this, for several days and nights, they had no annoyance whatsoever and began to think that the nuisance had expended itself. But on the night of the 13th September, Jane Easterbrook, an English maid, having gone into the pantry for the small silver bowl in which her mistress's bedtime drink was served, happening to look up at the little window of only four panes, observed through an auger-hole which was drilled through the window frame for the admission of a bolt to secure the shutter, a white pudgy finger – first the tip and then the two first joints introduced and turned about thus way and that, crooked against the inside, as if in search of a fastening which its owner destined to push aside. When the maid got back into the kitchen, we

are told,
"She fell into 'a
swound,' and was all
the next day very weak."

Mr. Prosser being, I've heard, a
hard-headed and conceited sort of
fellow, scouted the ghost and sneered at
the fears of his family. He was privately of the
opinion that the whole affair was a practical
joke or a fraud, and waited an opportunity of
catching the rogue in flagrante delicto. He did not long
keep this theory to himself, but let it out by degrees with
no stint of oaths and threats, believing that some domestic
traitor held the thread of the conspiracy.

Indeed it was time something were done; for not only his
servants, but good Mrs. Prosser herself, had grown to look
unhappy and anxious. They kept at home from the hour of
sunset and would not venture about the house after nightfall,
except in couples.

The knocking had ceased for about a week; when one
night, Mrs. Prosser being in the nursery, her husband, who
was in the parlor, heard it begin very softly at the hall door.
The air was quite still, which favored his hearing distinctly.
This was the first time there had been any disturbance at
that side of the house and the character of the summons
was changed.

Mr. Prosser, leaving the parlor door open it
seems, went quietly into the hall. The

sound was that of beating on the outside of the stout door, softly and regularly, "with the flat of the hand." He was going to open it suddenly, but changed his mind; and went back very quietly and on to the head of the kitchen stair, where was a "strong closet" over the pantry, in which he kept his firearms, swords, and canes.

Here he called his manservant, whom he believed to be honest, and with a pair of loaded pistols in his own coat pockets and giving another pair to him, he went as lightly as he could, followed by the man, and with a stout walking cane in his hand, forward to the door.

Everything went as Mr. Prosser wished. The besieger of his house, so far from taking fright at their approach, grew more impatient; and the sort of patting which had aroused his attention at first assumed the rhythm and emphasis of a series of double knocks.

Mr. Prosser, angry, opened the door with his right arm across, cane in hand. Looking, he saw nothing; but his arm was jerked up oddly, as it might be with the hollow of a hand, and something passed under it, with a kind of gentle squeeze. The servant neither saw nor felt anything, and did not know why his master looked back so hastily, cutting with his cane and shutting the door with so sudden a slam.

From that time Mr. Prosser discontinued his angry talk and swearing about it, and seemed nearly as averse from the subject as the rest of his family. He grew, in fact, very uncomfortable, feeling an inward persuasion that when, in answer to the summons, he had opened the hall door, he had actually given admission to the besieger.

He said nothing to Mrs. Prosser, but went up earlier to his bedroom, "where he read a while in his Bible, and said his prayers." I hope the particular relation of this circumstance does not indicate its singularity. He lay awake a good while, it appears; and, as he supposed, about a quarter past twelve he heard the soft palm of a hand patting on the outside of the bedroom door and then brushed slowly along it.

Up bounced Mr. Prosser, very much frightened, and locked the door, crying, "Who's there?" but receiving no answer, but the same brushing sound of a soft hand drawn over the panels, which he knew only too well.

In the morning the housemaid was terrified by the impression of a hand in the dust of the little parlour table, where they had been unpacking delft and other things the day before. The print of the naked foot in the sea sand did not frighten Robinson Crusoe half so much. They were by this time all nervous, and some of them half-crazed, about the hand.

Mr. Prosser went to examine the mark and made light of it, but, as he swore afterward, rather to quiet his servants than from any

38

comfortable feeling about it in his own mind. However, he had them all one by one into the room and made each place his or her hand, palm downward, on the same table, thus taking a similar impression from every person in the house, including himself and his wife. And his "affidavit" deposed that the formation of the hand so impressed differed altogether from those of the living inhabitants of the house and corresponded with that of the hand seen by Mrs. Prosser and by the cook.

Whoever or whatever the owner of that hand might be, they all felt his subtle demonstration to mean that it was declared he was no longer out of doors, but had established himself in the house.

And now Mrs. Prosser began to be troubled with strange and horrible dreams, some of which as set out in detail, in Aunt Rebecca's long letter, are really very appalling nightmares. But one night, as Mr. Prosser closed his bedchamber door, he was struck somewhat by the utter silence of the room, there being no sound of breathing, which seemed strange to him, as he knew his wife was in bed and his ears were particularly sharp.

There was a candle burning on a small table at the foot of the bed, besides the one he held in one hand, a heavy ledger, connected with his father-in-law's business being under his arm. He drew the curtain at the side of the bed and saw Mrs. Prosser lying – as for a few seconds he mortally feared – dead, her face being motionless, white, and covered with a cold dew; and on the pillow, close beside her head and just within the curtains, was as he first thought a toad – but really the same fattish hand, the wrist resting on the pillow and the fingers extended toward her temple.

Mr. Prosser, with a horrified jerk, pitched the ledger directly at the curtains, behind which the owner of the hand might be supposed to stand. The hand was instantaneously and smoothly snatched away, the curtains made a great wave, and Mr. Prosser got round the bed in time to see the closet door, which was at the other side, pulled to by the same white, puffy hand, as he believed.

He drew the door open with a fling and stared in, but the closet was empty, except for the clothes hanging from the pegs on the wall and the dressing table and looking glass facing the windows. He shut it sharply and locked it and felt for a minute, he says, "as if he were like to lose his wits." Then, ringing at the bell, he brought the servants, and, with much ado, they recovered Mrs. Prosser from a sort of "trance," in which, he says, from her looks, she seemed to have suffered "the pains of death," and Aunt Rebecca adds, "from what she told me of her visions, with her own lips, he might have added, 'and of hell also.'"

But the occurrence which seems to have determined the crisis was the strange sickness of their eldest child, a little boy aged between two and three years. He lay awake, seemingly in paroxysms of terror, and the doctors who were called in set down the symptoms to incipient water on the brain. Mrs. Prosser used to sit up with the nurse by the nursery fire, much troubled in mind about the condition of her child.

His
bed was
placed
sideways
along the wall,
with its head
against the door of
a press or cupboard
which, however, did
not shut quite close.
There was a little
valance about a
foot deep, round
the top of the child's
bed and this descended within some
ten or twelve inches of the pillow on which it lay.

They observed that the little creature was quieter whenever they took it up and held it on their laps. They had just replaced him, as he seemed to have grown quite sleepy and tranquil, but he was not five minutes in his bed when he began to scream in one of his frenzies of terror; at the same moment the nurse for the first time detected, and Mrs. Prosser equally plainly saw, following the direction of her eyes, the real cause of the child's sufferings.

Protruding through the aperture of the press and shrouded in the shade of the valance, they plainly saw the white fat hand, palm downward, presented toward the head of the child. The mother uttered a scream and snatched the child from its little bed, and she and the nurse ran down to the lady's sleeping room, where Mr. Prosser was in bed, shutting the door as they entered. They had hardly done so, when a gentle tap came to it from the outside.

There is a great deal more, but this will suffice. The singularity of the narrative seems to me to be this, that it describes the ghost of a hand and no more. The person to whom that hand belonged never once appeared; nor was it a hand separated from a body, but only a hand so manifested and introduced that its owner was always, by some crafty accident, hidden from view.

In the year 1819, at a college breakfast, I met a Mr. Prosser – a thin, grave, but rather chatty old gentleman, with very white hair drawn back into a pigtail – and he told us all, with a concise particularity, a story of his cousin, James Prosser, who, when an infant, had slept for some time in what his mother said was a haunted nursery in an old house near Chapelizod and who, whenever he was ill, over-fatigued, or in anywise feverish, suffered all through his life as he had done from a time he could scarce remember, from a vision of a certain gentleman, fat and pale, every curl of whose wig, every button and fold of whose laced clothes, and every feature and line of whose sensual, benignant, and unwholesome face, was as minutely engraven upon his memory as the dress and lineaments of his own grandfather's portrait, which hung before him every day at breakfast, dinner, and supper.

Mr. Prosser mentioned this as an instance of a curiously monotonous, individualized, and persistent nightmare and hinted the extreme horror and anxiety with which his cousin, of whom he spoke in the past tense as "poor Jemmie," was at any time induced to mention it.

I hope the reader will pardon me for loitering so long in the Tiled House, but this sort of lore has always had a charm for me; and people, you know – especially old people – will talk of what most interests themselves, too often forgetting that others may have had more than enough of it.

WUTHERING HEIGHTS

Emily Brontë

Extract

The business of eating being concluded, I approached a window to examine the weather. A sorrowful sight I saw: dark night coming down prematurely, and sky and hills mingled in one bitter whirl of wind and suffocating snow.

"I don't think it possible for me to get home now without a guide," I could not help exclaiming. "The roads will be buried already. Mrs. Heathcliff," I said earnestly, "you must excuse me for troubling you. I presume because, with that face, I'm sure you cannot help being good-hearted. Do point out some landmarks by which I may know my way home."

"Take the road you came," she answered, ensconcing herself in a chair, with a candle and the long book open before her. "It is brief advice, but as sound as I can give."

"Then, if you hear of me being discovered dead in a bog or a pit full of snow, your conscience won't whisper that it is partly your fault?"

"How so? I cannot escort you. They wouldn't let me go to the end of the garden wall."

"You! I should be sorry to ask you to cross the threshold, for my convenience, on such a night," I cried. "I want you to *tell* me my way, not to show it, or else to persuade Mr. Heathcliff to give me a guide."

"Who? There is himself, Earnshaw, Zillah, Joseph, and I."

"Are there no boys at the farm?"

"No; those are all."

"Then, it follows that I am compelled to stay."

"That you may settle with your host. I have nothing to do with it."

"I hope it will be a lesson to you to make no more rash journeys on these hills," cried Heathcliff's stern voice from the kitchen entrance. "As to staying here, I don't keep accommodations for visitors."

"I can sleep on a chair in this room," I replied.

"No, no! A stranger is a stranger, be he rich or poor: it will not suit me to permit anyone the range of the place while I am off guard!" said the unmannerly wretch.

With this insult, my patience was at an end. I uttered an expression of disgust and pushed past him into the yard, running against Earnshaw in my haste. It was so dark that I could not see the means of exit; and, as I wandered round, I heard another specimen of their civil behavior among each other. At first, the young man appeared about to befriend me.

"I'll go with him as far as the park," he said.

"You'll go with him to hell!" exclaimed his master, or whatever relation he bore. "And who is to look after the horses, eh?"

"A man's life is of more consequence than one evening's neglect of the horses; somebody must go," murmured Mrs. Heathcliff, more kindly than I expected.

"Not at your command!" retorted Hareton. "If you set store on him, you'd better be quiet."

"Then I hope his ghost will haunt you; and I hope Mr. Heathcliff will never get another tenant till the Grange is a ruin," she answered, sharply.

"Hearken, hearken, shoo's cursing on 'em!" muttered Joseph, toward whom I had been steering.

He sat within earshot, milking the cows by the light of a lantern, which I seized unceremoniously and, calling out that I would send it back on the morrow, rushed to the nearest postern.

"Maister, maister, he's staling t' lantern!" shouted the ancient, pursuing my retreat. "Hey, Gnasher! Hey, dog! Hey Wolf, holld him, holld him!"

On opening the little door, two hairy monsters flew at my throat, bearing me down, and extinguishing the light; while a mingled guffaw from Heathcliff and Hareton put the copestone on my rage and humiliation.

Fortunately, the beasts seemed more bent on stretching their paws, and yawning, and flourishing their tails, than devouring me alive; but they would suffer no resurrection, and I was forced to lie till their malignant masters pleased to deliver me. Then, hatless and trembling with wrath, I ordered the miscreants to let me out – on their peril to keep me one minute longer – with several incoherent threats of retaliation that, in their indefinite depth of virulency, smacked of King Lear.

The vehemence of my agitation brought on a copious bleeding at the nose. Still Heathcliff laughed, and still I scolded. I don't know what would have concluded the scene, had there not been one person at hand rather more rational than myself, and more benevolent than my entertainer. This was Zillah, the stout housewife; who at length issued forth to inquire into the nature of the uproar. She thought that some of them had been laying violent hands on me; and, not daring to attack her master, she turned her vocal artillery against the younger scoundrel.

"Well, Mr. Earnshaw," she cried, "I wonder what you'll have agait next? Are we going to murder folk on our very door-stones? I see this house will never do for me – look at t' poor lad, he's fair choking! Wisht, wisht; you mun'n't go on so. Come in, and I'll cure that: there now, hold ye still."

With these words she suddenly splashed a pint of icy water down my neck, and pulled me into the kitchen. Mr. Heathcliff followed, his accidental merriment expiring quickly.

I was sick exceedingly, and dizzy, and faint; and thus compelled perforce to accept lodgings under his roof. He told Zillah to give me a glass of brandy, and then passed on to the inner room; while she condoled with me on my sorry predicament, and having obeyed his orders, whereby I was somewhat revived, ushered me to bed.

While leading the way upstairs, she recommended that I should hide the candle, and not make a noise; for her master had an odd notion about the chamber she would put me in, and never let anybody lodge there willingly. I asked the reason. She did not know, she answered; she had only lived there a year or two, and they had so many queer goings on, she could not begin to be curious.

Too stupefied to be curious myself, I fastened my door and glanced round for the bed. The whole furniture consisted of a chair, a clothespress, and a large oak case with squares cut out near the top resembling coach windows. Having approached this structure, I looked inside and perceived it to be a singular sort of old-fashioned couch, very conveniently designed to obviate the necessity for every member of the family having a room to himself. In fact, it formed a little closet, and the ledge of a window, which it enclosed, served as a table. I slid back the panelled sides, pulled them together again, and felt secure against the vigilance of Heathcliff, and everyone else.

The ledge, where I placed my candle, had a few mildewed books piled up in one corner; and it was covered with writing scratched on the wood. This writing, however, was nothing but a name repeated in all kinds of characters, large and small – "Catherine Earnshaw," here and there varied to "Catherine Heathcliff," and then again to "Catherine Linton."

In vapid listlessness I leaned my head against the window, and continued spelling over Catherine Earnshaw – Heathcliff –

Linton, till my eyes closed; but they had not rested five minutes when a glare of white letters started from the dark – the air swarmed with Catherines; and rousing myself to dispel the obtrusive name, I discovered my candle-wick reclining on one of the antique volumes, and perfuming the place with an odor of roasted calf-skin. I snuffed it off, and, very ill at ease under the influence of cold and nausea, sat up and spread open the injured tome on my knee. It was a Testament, in lean type, and smelling dreadfully musty; a fly-leaf bore the inscription – "Catherine Earnshaw, her book," and a date some quarter of a century back. I shut it, and took up another and another, till I had examined all. Catherine's library was select, and its state of dilapidation proved it to have been well used, though not altogether for a legitimate purpose: scarcely one chapter had escaped a pen-and-ink commentary – at least the appearance of one – covering every morsel of blank that the printer had left. Some were detached sentences; other parts took the form of a regular diary, scrawled in an unformed, childish hand. At the top of an extra page (quite a treasure, probably, when first lighted on), I was greatly amused to behold an excellent caricature of my friend Joseph – rudely, yet powerfully sketched. An immediate interest kindled within me for the unknown Catherine, and I began forthwith to decipher her faded hieroglyphics.

"An awful Sunday," commenced the paragraph beneath. "I wish my father were back again. Hindley is a detestable substitute – his conduct to Heathcliff is atrocious. H and I are going to rebel – we took our initiatory step this evening.

"All day had been flooding with rain; we could not go to church, so Joseph must needs get up a congregation in the garret; and, while Hindley and his wife basked downstairs before a comfortable fire – doing anything but reading their Bibles, I'll answer for it – Heathcliff, myself, and the unhappy ploughboy were commanded to take our prayer books, and mount. We were ranged in a row on a sack of corn, groaning and shivering, and hoping that Joseph would shiver too, so that he might give us a short homily for his own sake. A vain idea! The service lasted precisely three hours; and yet my brother had the face to exclaim, when he saw us descending, 'What, done already?' On Sunday evenings we used to be permitted to play, if we did not make much noise; now a mere titter is sufficient to send us into corners.

"'You forget you have a master here,' says the tyrant. 'I'll demolish the first who puts me out of temper! I insist on perfect sobriety and silence. Oh, boy! was that you? Frances darling, pull his hair as you go by; I heard him snap his fingers.' Frances pulled his hair heartily and then went and seated herself on her husband's knee, and there they were, like two babies, kissing and talking nonsense by the hour – foolish palaver that we should be ashamed of. We made ourselves as snug as our means allowed in the arch of the dresser. I had just fastened our pinafores together and hung them up for a curtain, when in comes Joseph, on an errand from the stables. He tears down my handiwork, boxes my ears, and croaks:

"'T' maister nobbut just buried, and Sabbath not o'ered, und t' sound o' t' gospel still i' yer lugs, and ye darr be laiking! Shame on ye! sit ye down, ill childer! There's good books eneugh if ye'll read 'em: sit ye down, and think o' yer sowls!'

"Saying this, he compelled us so to square our positions that we might receive from the far-off fire a dull ray to show us the text of the lumber he thrust upon us. I could not bear the employment. I took my dingy volume by the scroop, and hurled it into the dog kennel, vowing I hated a good book. Heathcliff kicked his to the same place. Then there was a hubbub!

"'Maister Hindley!' shouted our chaplain. 'Maister, coom hither! Miss Cathy's riven th' back off "Th' Helmet o' Salvation," un' Heathcliff's pawsed his fit into t' first part o' "T' Brooad Way to Destruction!" It's fair flaysome that ye let 'em go on this gait. Ech! Th' owd man wad ha' laced 'em properly – but he's goan!'

"Hindley hurried up from his paradise on the hearth, and seizing one of us by the collar and the other by the arm, hurled both into the back-kitchen; where, Joseph asseverated, "owd Nick" would fetch us as sure as we were living: and, so comforted, we each sought a separate nook to await his advent.

"I reached this book, and a pot of ink from a shelf, and pushed the house door ajar to give me light, and I have got the time on with writing for twenty minutes. But my companion is impatient, and proposes that we should appropriate the dairywoman's cloak, and have a scamper on the moors, under its shelter. A pleasant suggestion – and then, if the surly old man come in, he may believe his prophecy verified: we cannot be damper, or colder, in the rain than we are here."

I suppose Catherine fulfilled her project, for the next sentence took up another subject: she waxed lachrymose.

"How little did I dream that Hindley would ever make me cry so!" she wrote. "My head aches, till I cannot keep it on the pillow; and still I can't give over. Poor Heathcliff! Hindley calls him a vagabond, and won't let him sit with us, nor eat with us any more; and, he says, he and I must not play together, and threatens to turn him out of the house if we break his orders. He has been blaming our father (how dared he?) for treating H too liberally; and swears he will reduce him to his right place—"

I began to nod drowsily over the dim page: my eye wandered from manuscript to print. I saw a red ornamented title: *Seventy Times Seven, and the First of the Seventy-First. A Pious Discourse delivered by the Reverend Jabez Branderham, in the Chapel of Gimmerden Sough.* And while I was, half consciously, worrying my brain to guess what Jabez Branderham would make of his subject, I sank back in bed, and fell asleep. Alas, for the effects of bad tea and bad temper! What else could it be that made me pass such a terrible night?

I began to dream, almost before I ceased to be sensible of my locality. I thought it was morning; and I had set out on my way home, with Joseph for a guide. The snow lay yards deep in our road; and, as we floundered on, my companion wearied me with constant reproaches that I had not brought a pilgrim's staff: telling me that I could never get into the house without one, and boastfully flourishing a heavy-headed cudgel, which I understood to be so denominated. For a moment I considered it absurd that I should need such a weapon to gain admittance into my own residence. Then a new idea flashed across me. I was not going there: we were journeying to hear the famous Jabez Branderham preach, from the text – *Seventy Times Seven*; and either Joseph, the preacher, or I had committed the "First of the Seventy-First," and were to be publicly exposed and excommunicated.

We came to the chapel. I have passed it really in my walks, twice or thrice; it lies in a hollow, between two hills: an elevated hollow, near a swamp, whose peaty moisture is said to answer all the purposes of embalming on the few corpses deposited there. The roof has been kept whole hitherto; but as the clergyman's stipend is only twenty pounds per annum, and a house with two rooms, threatening speedily to determine into one, no clergyman will undertake the duties of pastor: especially as it is currently reported that his flock would rather let him starve than increase the living by one penny from their own pockets. However, in my dream, Jabez had a full and attentive congregation; and he preached – good God! What a sermon! Divided into *four hundred and ninety* parts, each fully equal to an ordinary address from the pulpit, and each discussing a separate sin! Where he searched for them, I cannot tell. He had his private manner of interpreting the phrase, and it seemed necessary the brother should sin different sins on every occasion.

Oh, how weary I grew. How I writhed, and yawned, and nodded, and revived! How I pinched and pricked myself, and rubbed my eyes, and stood up, and sat down again, and nudged Joseph to inform me if he would ever have done. I was condemned to hear all out: finally, he reached the "First of the Seventy-First." At that crisis, a sudden inspiration descended on me; I was moved to rise and denounce Jabez Branderham as the sinner of the sin that no Christian need pardon.

"Sir," I exclaimed, "sitting here within these four walls, at one stretch, I have endured and forgiven the four hundred and ninety heads of your discourse. Seventy times seven times have I plucked up my hat and been about to depart – seventy times seven times have you preposterously forced me to resume my seat. The four hundred and ninety-first is too much. Fellow-martyrs, have at him! Drag him down, and crush him to atoms, that the place which knows him may know him no more!"

"*Thou art the man!*" cried Jabez, after a solemn pause, leaning over his cushion. "Seventy times seven times didst thou gapingly contort thy visage – seventy times seven did I take counsel with my soul. Lo, this is human weakness: this also may be absolved! The First of the Seventy-First is come. Brethren, execute upon him the judgment written. Such honor have all His saints!"

With that concluding word, the whole assembly, exalting their pilgrim's staves, rushed round me in a body; and I, having no weapon to raise in self-defence, commenced grappling with Joseph, my nearest and most ferocious assailant, for his. In the confluence of the multitude, several clubs crossed; blows, aimed at me, fell on other skulls. Presently the whole chapel resounded with rappings and counter rappings: every man's hand was against his neighbor; and Branderham, unwilling to remain idle, poured forth his zeal in a shower of loud taps on the boards of the pulpit, which responded so smartly that, at last, to my unspeakable relief, they woke me.

And what was it that had suggested the tremendous tumult? What had played Jabez's part in the row? Merely the branch of a fir tree that touched my lattice as the blast wailed by, and rattled its dry cones against the panes! I listened doubtingly an instant; detected the disturber, then turned and dozed, and dreamt again: if possible, still more disagreeably than before.

This time, I remembered I was lying in the oak closet, and I heard distinctly the gusty wind, and the driving of the snow. I heard, also, the fir bough repeat its teasing sound, and ascribed it to the right cause, but it annoyed me so much that I resolved to silence it, if possible; and I thought I rose and endeavored to unhasp the casement. The hook was soldered into the staple: a circumstance observed by me when awake, but forgotten. "I must stop it, nevertheless!" I muttered, knocking my knuckles through the glass, and stretching an arm out to seize the importunate branch; instead of which, my fingers closed on the fingers of a little, ice-cold hand!

The intense horror of nightmare came over me: I tried to draw back my arm, but the hand clung to it, and a most melancholy voice sobbed, "Let me in – let me in!"

"Who are you?" I asked, struggling, meanwhile, to disengage myself.

"Catherine Linton," it replied, shiveringly (why did I think of Linton? I had read 'Earnshaw' twenty times for Linton).

56

"I'm come home – I'd lost my way on the moor!"

As it spoke, I discerned, obscurely, a child's face looking through the window. Terror made me cruel; and, finding it useless to attempt shaking the creature off, I pulled its wrist onto the broken pane, and rubbed it to and fro till the blood ran down and soaked the bedclothes. Still it wailed, "Let me in!" and maintained its tenacious gripe, almost maddening me with fear.

"How can I!" I said at length. "Let me go, if you want me to let you in!"

The fingers relaxed, I snatched mine through the hole, hurriedly piled the books up in a pyramid against it, and stopped my ears to exclude the lamentable prayer.

"If the little fiend had got in at the window, she probably would have strangled me!" I returned. "I'm not going to endure the persecutions of your hospitable ancestors again. Was not the Reverend Jabez Branderham akin to you on the mother's side? And that minx, Catherine Linton, or Earnshaw, or however she was called – she must have been a changeling – wicked little soul! She told me she had been walking the earth these twenty years: a just punishment for her mortal transgressions, I've no doubt!"

Scarcely were these words uttered when I recollected the association of Heathcliff's with Catherine's name in the book, which had completely slipped from my memory, till thus awakened. I blushed at my inconsideration, but, without showing further consciousness of the offence, I hastened to add:

"The truth is, sir, I passed the first part of the night in—" Here I stopped afresh – I was about to say "perusing those old volumes," then it would have revealed my knowledge of their written, as well as their printed, contents; so, correcting myself, I went on, "in spelling over the name scratched on that window ledge. A monotonous occupation, calculated to set me asleep, like counting, or—"

"What can you mean by talking in this way to me!" thundered Heathcliff with savage vehemence. "How – how dare you, under my roof? God! He's mad to speak so!" And he struck his forehead with rage.

I did not know whether to resent this language or pursue my explanation; but he seemed so powerfully affected that

I took pity and proceeded with my dreams, affirming I had never heard the appellation of "Catherine Linton" before, but reading it often over produced an impression which personified itself when I had no longer my imagination under control. Heathcliff gradually fell back into the shelter of the bed as I spoke, finally sitting down almost concealed behind it. I guessed, however, by his irregular and intercepted breathing, that he struggled to vanquish an excess of violent emotion. Not liking to show him that I had heard the conflict, I continued my toilette rather noisily, looked at my watch, and soliloquised on the length of the night: "Not three o'clock yet! I could have taken oath it had been six. Time stagnates here – we must surely have retired to rest at eight!"

"Always at nine in winter, and rise at four," said my host, suppressing a groan and, as I fancied, by the motion of his arm's shadow, dashing a tear from his eyes. "Mr. Lockwood," he added, "you may go into my room: you'll only be in the way, coming downstairs so early; and your childish outcry has sent sleep to the devil for me."

"And for me, too," I replied. "I'll walk in the yard till daylight, and then I'll be off; and you need not dread a repetition of my intrusion. I'm now quite cured of seeking pleasure in society, be it country or town. A sensible man ought to find sufficient company in himself."

"Delightful company!" muttered Heathcliff. "Take the candle, and go where you please. I shall join you directly. Keep out of the yard, though, the dogs are unchained; and the house – Juno mounts sentinel there, and – nay, you can

It opened into the house, where the females were already astir – Zillah urging flakes of flame up the chimney with a colossal bellows, and Mrs. Heathcliff, kneeling on the hearth, reading a book by the aid of the blaze. She held her hand interposed between the furnace heat and her eyes, and seemed absorbed in her occupation; desisting from it only to chide the servant for covering her with sparks, or to push away a dog, now and then, that snoozled its nose overforwardly into her face. I was surprised to see Heathcliff there also. He stood by the fire, his back toward me, just finishing a stormy scene with poor Zillah, who ever and anon interrupted her labor to pluck up the corner of her apron and heave an indignant groan.

"And you, you worthless—" he broke out as I entered, turning to his daughter-in-law, and employing an epithet as harmless as duck, or sheep, but generally represented by a dash. "There you are, at your idle tricks again! The rest of them do earn their bread – you live on my charity! Put your trash away, and find something to do. You shall pay me for the plague of having you eternally in my sight – do you hear, damnable jade?"

"I'll put my trash away, because you can make me if I refuse," answered the young lady, closing her book and throwing it on a chair. "But I'll not do anything, though you should swear your tongue out, except what I please!"

64

Heathcliff lifted his hand, and the speaker sprang to a safer distance, obviously acquainted with its weight.

Having no desire to be entertained by a cat-and-dog combat, I stepped forward briskly, as if eager to partake the warmth of the hearth, and innocent of any knowledge of the interrupted dispute. Each had enough decorum to suspend further hostilities. Heathcliff placed his fists, out of temptation, in his pockets; Mrs. Heathcliff curled her lip and walked to a seat far off, where she kept her word by playing the part of a statue during the remainder of my stay.

THE HAUNTED DOLL'S HOUSE

M. R. James

Mr. Dillet pointed with his stick to an object which shall be described when the time comes and said, "I suppose you get stuff of that kind through your hands pretty often?" And when he said it, he lied in his throat and knew that he lied. Not once in twenty years – perhaps not once in a lifetime – could Mr. Chittenden, skilled as he was in ferreting out the forgotten treasures of half a dozen counties, expect to handle such a specimen. It was a collector's palaver, and Mr. Chittenden recognized it as such.

"Stuff of that kind, Mr. Dillet! It's a museum piece, that is."

"Well, I suppose there are museums that'll take anything."

"I've seen one, not as good as that, years back," said Mr. Chittenden, thoughtfully. "But that's not likely to come into the market, and I'm told they 'ave some fine ones of the period over the water. No, I'm only telling you the truth, Mr. Dillet, when I say that if you was to place an unlimited order with me for the very best that could be got – and you know I 'ave facilities for getting to know of such things and a reputation to maintain – well, all I can say is, I should lead you straight up to that one and say, 'I can't do no better for you than that, sir.'"

"Hear, hear!" said Mr. Dillet, applauding ironically with the end of his stick on the floor of the shop. "How much are you sticking the innocent American buyer for it, eh?"

"Oh, I shan't be over hard on the buyer, American or otherwise. You see, it stands this way, Mr. Dillet – if I knew just a bit more about the pedigree—"

"Or just a bit less," Mr. Dillet put in.

"Ha, ha! You will have your joke, sir. No, but as I was saying, if I knew just a little more than what I do about the piece – though anyone can see for themselves it's a genuine thing, every last corner of it, and there's not been one of my men allowed to so much as touch it since it came into the shop – there'd be another figure in the price I'm asking."

"And what's that – five and twenty?"

"Multiply that by three and you've got it, sir. Seventy-five's my price."

"And fifty's mine," said Mr. Dillet.

The point of agreement was, of course, somewhere between the two, it does not matter exactly where – I think sixty guineas. But half an hour later the object was being packed, and within an hour Mr. Dillet had called for it in his car and driven away. Mr. Chittenden, holding the check in his hand, saw him off from the door with smiles and returned, still smiling, into the parlor where his wife was making the tea. He stopped at the door.

"It's gone," he said.

"Thank God for that!" said Mrs. Chittenden, putting down the teapot. "Mr. Dillet, was it?"

"Yes, it was."

"Well, I'd sooner it was him than another."

"Oh, I don't know, he ain't a bad fellow, my dear."

"Maybe not, but in my opinion he'd be none the worse for a bit of a shake up."

"Well, if that's your opinion, it's my opinion he's put himself into the way of getting one. Anyhow, we shan't have no more of it and that's something to be thankful for."

And so Mr. and Mrs. Chittenden sat down to tea.

And what of Mr. Dillet and of his new acquisition? What it was, the title of this story will have told you. What it was like, I shall have to indicate as well as I can.

There was only just room enough for it in the car and Mr. Dillet had to sit with the driver. He had also to go slow, for though the rooms of the Dolls' House had all been stuffed carefully with soft cotton wool, jolting was to be avoided, in view of the immense number of small objects which thronged them; and the ten-mile drive was an anxious time for him, in spite of all the precautions he insisted upon. At last his front door was reached and Collins, the butler, came out.

"Look here, Collins, you must help me with this thing – it's a delicate job. We must get it out upright, see? It's full of little things that mustn't be displaced more than we can help. Let's see, where shall we have it?" He paused, considering. "Really, I think I shall have to put it in my own room, to begin with at any rate. On the big table – that's it."

It was conveyed – with much talking – to Mr. Dillet's spacious room on the first floor, looking out on the drive. The sheeting was unwound from it and the front thrown open, and for the next hour or two Mr Dillet was fully occupied in extracting the padding and setting in order the contents of the rooms.

When this thoroughly congenial task was finished, I must say that it would have been difficult to find a more perfect and attractive specimen of a Dolls' House in Strawberry Hill Gothic than that which now stood on Mr. Dillet's large kneehole table, lighted up by the evening sun which came slanting through three tall sash-windows.

It was quite six feet long, including the chapel or oratory which flanked the front on the left as you faced it, and the stable on the right. The main block of the house was, as I have said, in the Gothic manner; that is to say, the windows had pointed arches and were surmounted by what are called ogival hoods, with crockets and finials such as we see on the canopies of tombs built into church walls. At the angles were absurd turrets covered with arched panels. The chapel had pinnacles and buttresses and a bell in the turret and colored glass in the windows. When the front of the house was open you saw four large rooms – bedroom, dining room, drawing room, and kitchen – each with its appropriate furniture in a very complete state.

The stable on the right was in two stories, with its proper complement of horses, coaches, and grooms, and with its clock and Gothic cupola for the clock bell.

Pages, of course, might be written on the outfit of the mansion – how many frying pans, how many gilt chairs, what pictures, carpets, chandeliers, four-posters, table linen, glass, crockery and plate it possessed; but all this must be left to the imagination. I will only say that the base or plinth on which the house stood (for it was fitted with one of some depth which allowed for a flight of steps to the front door and a terrace, partly balustraded) contained a shallow drawer or drawers in which were neatly stored sets of embroidered curtains, changes of raiment for the inmates and, in short, all the materials for an infinite series of variations and refittings of the most absorbing and delightful kind.

"Quintessence of Horace Walpole, that's what it is. He must have had something to do with the making of it." Such was Mr. Dillet's murmured reflection as he knelt before it in a reverent ecstasy. "Simply wonderful; this is my day and no mistake. Five hundred pounds coming in this morning for that cabinet which I never cared about, and now this tumbling into my hands for a tenth, at the very most, of what it would fetch in town. Well, well! It almost makes one afraid something'll happen to counter it. Let's have a look at the population, anyhow."

Accordingly he set them before him in a row. Again, here is an opportunity, which some would snatch at, of making an inventory of costume: I am incapable of it.

There were a gentleman and lady, in blue satin and brocade respectively. There were two children, a boy and a girl. There was a cook, a nurse, a footman, and there were the stable servants – two postillions, a coachman, two grooms.

"Anyone else? Yes, possibly."

The curtains of the four-poster in the bedroom were closely drawn round four sides of it and he put his fingerin between them and felt in the bed. He drew the finger back hastily, for it almost seemed to him as if something had – not stirred, perhaps, but yielded – in an odd, live way as he pressed it. Then he put back the curtains, which ran on rods in the proper manner, and extracted from the bed a white-haired old gentleman in a long linen nightdress and cap, and laid him down by the rest. The tale was complete.

Dinner time was now near, so Mr. Dillet spent but five minutes in putting the lady and children into the drawing room, the gentleman into the dining room, the servants into the kitchen and stables, and the old man back into his bed. He retired into his dressing room next door and we see or hear no more of him until something like one o'clock at night.

His whim was to sleep surrounded by some of the gems of his collection. The big room in which we have seen him contained his bed. Bath, wardrobe, and all the appliances of dressing were in a commodious room adjoining; but his four-poster, which itself was a valued treasure, stood in the large room where he sometimes wrote and often sat and received visitors. Tonight he repaired to it in a highly complacent frame of mind.

There was no striking clock within earshot – none on the staircase, none in the stable, none in the distant church tower. Yet it is indubitable that Mr. Dillet was startled out of a very pleasant slumber by a bell tolling one.

He was so much startled that he did not merely lie breathlessly with wide-open eyes, but actually sat up in his bed.

He never asked himself, till the morning hours, how it was that, though there was no light at all in the room, the Dolls' House on the kneehole table stood out with complete clearness. But it was so. The effect was that of a bright harvest moon shining full on the front of a big white stone mansion – a quarter of a mile away it might be and yet every detail was photographically sharp. There were trees about it too – trees rising behind the chapel and the house. He seemed to be conscious of the scent of a cool, still September night. He thought he could hear an occasional stamp and clink from the stables, as of horses stirring. And with another shock he realized that, above the house, he was looking – not at the wall of his room – but into the profound blue of a night sky.

There were lights, more than one, in the windows, and he quickly saw that this was no four-roomed house with a movable front, but one of many rooms and staircases – a real house, but seen as if through the wrong end of a telescope. "You mean to show me something," he muttered to himself, and he gazed earnestly on the lighted windows. They would in real life have been shuttered or curtained, no doubt, he thought; but as it was there was nothing to intercept his view of what was being transacted inside the rooms.

Two rooms were lighted – one on the ground floor to the right of the door, one upstairs on the left – the first brightly enough, the other rather dimly. The lower room was the dining room – a table was laid, but the meal was over and only wine and glasses were left on the table. The man of the blue satin and the woman of the brocade were alone in the room and they were talking very earnestly, seated close together at the table, their elbows on it – every now and again stopping to listen, as it seemed. Once he rose, came to the window and opened it and put his head out and his hand to his ear. There was a lighted taper in a silver candlestick on a sideboard. When the man left the window he seemed to leave the room also; and the lady, taper in hand, remained standing and listening. The expression on her face was that of one striving her utmost to keep down a fear that threatened to master her – and succeeding. It was a hateful face, too: broad, flat, and sly. Now the man came back and she took some small thing from him and hurried out of the room. He too, disappeared, but only for a moment or two. The front door slowly opened and he stepped out and stood on the top of the perron, looking this way and that, then turned toward the upper window that was lighted and shook his fist.

It was time to look at that upper window. Through it was seen a four-poster bed: a nurse or other servant in an armchair, evidently sound asleep; in the bed an old man lying: awake and, one would say, anxious, from the way in which he shifted about and moved his fingers, beating tunes on the coverlet. Beyond the bed a door opened. Light was seen on the ceiling and the lady came in: she set down her candle on a table, came to the fireside and roused the nurse. In her hand she had an old-fashioned wine bottle, ready uncorked. The nurse took it, poured some of the contents into a little silver saucepan, added some spice and sugar from casters on the table, and set it to warm on the fire. Meanwhile the old man in the bed beckoned feebly to the lady, who came to him, smiling, took his wrist as if to feel his pulse and bit her lip as if in consternation. He looked at her anxiously and then pointed to the window and spoke. She nodded and did as the man below had done; opened the casement and listened, perhaps rather ostentatiously, then drew her head in and shook it, looking at the old man, who seemed to sigh.

By this time the posset on the fire was steaming and the nurse poured it into a small two-handled silver bowl and brought it to the bedside. The old man seemed disinclined for it and was waving it away, but the lady and the nurse together bent over him and evidently pressed it upon him. He must have yielded, for they supported him into a sitting position and put it to his lips. He drank most of it, in several drafts, and they laid him down. The lady left the room, smiling goodnight to him, and took the bowl, the bottle, and the silver saucepan with her. The nurse returned to the chair and there was an interval of complete quiet.

Suddenly the old man started up in his bed – and he must have uttered some cry, for the nurse started out of her chair and made but one step of it to the bedside. He was a sad and terrible sight – flushed in the face, almost to blackness, the eyes glaring whitely, both hands clutching at his heart, foam at his lips.

For a moment the nurse left him, ran to the door, flung

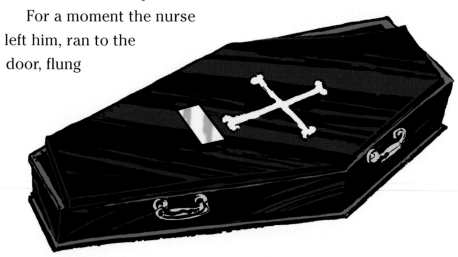

it wide open, and one supposes, screamed aloud for help, then darted back to the bed and seemed to try feverishly to soothe him – to lay him down – anything. But as the lady, her husband, and several servants rushed into the room with horrified faces, the old man collapsed under the nurse's hands and lay back and the features, contorted with agony and rage, relaxed slowly into calm.

A few moments later, lights showed out to the left of the house and a coach with flambeaux drove up to the door. A white-wigged man in black got nimbly out and ran up the steps, carrying a small, leather, trunk-shaped box. He was met in the doorway by the man and his wife, she with her handkerchief clutched between her hands, he with a tragic face, but retaining his self-control. They led the newcomer into the dining room, where he set his box of papers on the table and, turning to them, listened with a face of consternation at what they had to tell. He nodded his head again and again, threw out his hands slightly, declined, it seemed, offers of refreshment and lodging for the night, and within a few minutes came slowly down the steps, entering the coach and driving off the way he had come. As the man in blue watched him from the top of the steps, a smile not pleasant to see stole slowly over his fat white face. Darkness fell over the whole scene as the lights of the coach disappeared.

But Mr. Dillet remained sitting up in the bed; he had rightly guessed that there would be a sequel. The house front glimmered out again before long. But now there was a difference. The lights were in other windows, one at the top of the house, the other illuminating the range of colored windows of the chapel. How he saw through these is not quite obvious, but he did. The interior was as carefully furnished as the rest of the establishment, with its minute red cushions on the desks, its Gothic stall-canopies, and its western gallery and pinnacled organ with gold pipes. On the center of the black and white pavement was a bier: four tall candles burned at the corners. On the bier was a coffin covered with a pall of black velvet.

As he looked the folds of the pall stirred. It seemed to rise at one end: it slid downward: it fell away, exposing the black coffin with its silver handles and nameplate. One of the tall candlesticks swayed and toppled over. Ask no more, but turn, as Mr. Dillet hastily did, and look in at the lighted window at the top of the house, where a boy and girl lay in two truckle beds, and a four-poster for the nurse rose above them. The nurse was not visible for the moment; but the father and mother were there, now in mourning, but with very little sign of mourning in their demeanor. Indeed, they were laughing and talking with a good deal of animation, sometimes to each other and sometimes throwing a remark to one or other of the children and again laughing at the answers. Then the father was seen to go on tiptoe out of the room, taking with him as he went a white garment that hung on a peg near the door. He shut the door after him. A minute or two later it was slowly opened again and a muffled head poked round it. A bent form of sinister shape stepped across to the truckle beds and suddenly stopped, threw up its arms and revealed, of course, the father, laughing. The children were in agonies of terror, the boy with the bedclothes over his head, the girl throwing herself out of bed into her mother's arms. Attempts at consolation followed – the parents took the children on their laps, patted them, picked up the white gown and showed there was no harm in it and so forth; and at last putting the children back into bed, left the room with encouraging waves of the hand. As they left it, the nurse came in and soon the light died down.

Still Mr. Dillet watched immovable.

A new sort of light – not of lamp or candle – a pale ugly light, began to dawn around the door-case at the back of the room. The door was opening again. The seer does not like to dwell upon what he saw entering the room. He says it might be described as a frog – the size of a man – but it had scanty white hair about its head. It was busy about the truckle beds, but not for long. The sound of cries – faint, as if coming out of a vast distance – but even so, infinitely appalling, reached the ear. There were signs of a hideous commotion all over the house: lights passed along and up, and doors opened and shut, and running figures passed within the windows. The clock in the stable turret tolled one and darkness fell again.

It was only dispelled once more, to show the house front. At the bottom of the steps dark figures were drawn up in two lines, holding flaming torches. More dark figures came down the steps, bearing, first one, then another small coffin. And the lines of torch bearers, with the coffins between them, moved silently onward to the left.

The hours of night passed on – never so slowly, Mr. Dillet thought. Gradually he sank down from sitting to lying in his bed, but he did not close an eye, and early next morning he sent for the doctor.

The doctor found him in a disquieting state of nerves and recommended sea air. To a quiet place on the east coast he accordingly repaired by easy stages in his car.

One of the first people he met on the sea front was Mr. Chittenden, who, it appeared, had likewise been advised to take his wife away for a bit of a change.

Mr. Chittenden looked somewhat askance upon him when they met, and not without cause.

"Well, I don't wonder at you being a bit upset, Mr. Dillet. What? Yes, well, I might say 'orrible upset, to be sure, seeing what me and my poor wife went through ourselves. But I put it to you, Mr. Dillet, one of two things: was I going to scrap a lovely piece like that on the one 'and, or was I going to tell customers, 'I'm selling you a regular picture-palace-drama in real life of the olden time, billed to perform regular at one o'clock a.m.?' Why, what would you 'ave said yourself? And next thing you know, two Justices of the Peace in the back parlor and poor Mr. and Mrs. Chittenden off in a spring cart to the County Asylum and everyone in the street saying, 'Ah, I thought it 'ud come to that. Look at the way the man drank!' – and me next door, or next door but one, to a total abstainer, as you know. Well, there was my position. What? Me 'ave it back in the shop? Well, what do you think? No, but I'll tell you what I will do. You shall have your money back, bar the ten pound I paid for it, and you make what you can."

Later in the day, in what is offensively called the "smoke room" of the hotel, a murmured conversation between the two went on for some time.

"How much do you really know about that thing and where it came from?"

"Honest, Mr. Dillet, I don't know the 'ouse. Of course, it came out of the lumber room of a country 'ouse – that anyone could guess. But I'll go as far as say this, that I believe it's not a hundred miles from this place. Which direction and how far I've no notion; I'm only judging by guesswork. The man as I actually paid the check to ain't one of my regular men and I've lost sight of him; but I 'ave the idea that this part of the country was his beat and that's every word I can tell you. But now, Mr. Dillet, there's one thing that rather physicks me. That old chap – I suppose you saw him drive up to the door – I thought so: now, would he have been the medical man, do you take it? My wife would have it so, but I stuck to it that was the lawyer, because he had papers with him and one he took out was folded up."

"I agree," said Mr. Dillet. "Thinking it over, I came to the conclusion that was the old man's will, ready to be signed."

"Just what I thought," said Mr. Chittenden, "and I took it that will would have cut out the young people, eh? Well, well! It's been a lesson to me, I know that. I shan't buy no more dolls' houses, nor waste no more money on the pictures – and as to this business of poisonin' grandpa, well, if I know myself, I never 'ad much of a turn for that. Live and let live: that's bin my motto throughout life and I ain't found it a bad one, that's for sure."

Filled with these elevated sentiments, Mr. Chittenden retired to his lodgings. Mr. Dillet next day repaired to the local Institute, where he hoped to find some clue to the riddle that absorbed him. He gazed in despair at a long file of the Canterbury and York Society's publications of the Parish Registers of the district. No print resembling the house of his nightmare was among those that hung on the staircase and in the passages. Disconsolate, he found himself in a derelict room, staring at a dusty model of a church in a dark and dusty glass case:

"Model of St. Stephen's Church, Coxham. Presented by J. Merewether, Esq., of Ilbridge House, 1877. The work of his ancestor James Merewether, d. 1786."

There was something in the fashion of it that reminded him dimly of his horror. He retraced his steps to a wall map he had noticed, and made out that Ilbridge House was in Coxham Parish. Coxham was, as it happened, one of the parishes of which he had retained the name when he glanced over the file of printed registers and it was not long before he found in them the record of the burial of Roger Milford, aged

76, on the 11th September 1757, and of Roger and Elizabeth Merewether, aged nine and seven, on the 19th of the same month. It seemed worthwhile to follow up this clue, frail as it was, and in the afternoon he drove out to Coxham. The east end of the north aisle of the church is a Milford chapel and on its north wall are tablets to the same persons; Roger, the elder, it seems, was distinguished by all the qualities which adorn "the Father, the Magistrate, and the Man." The memorial was erected by his attached daughter Elizabeth, "who did not long survive the loss of a parent ever solicitous for her welfare, and of two amiable children." The last sentence was plainly an addition to the original inscription.

A yet later slab told of James Merewether, husband of Elizabeth, "who in the dawn of life practised, not without success, those arts which, had he continued their exercise, might in the opinion of the most competent judges have earned for him the name of the British Vitruvius; but who, overwhelmed by the visitation which deprived him of an affectionate partner and a blooming offspring, passed his Prime and Age in a secluded yet elegant Retirement. His grateful Nephew and Heir indulges a pious sorrow by this too brief recital of his excellences."

The children were more simply commemorated. Both died on the night of the 12th of September.

Mr. Dillet felt sure that in Ilbridge House he had found the scene of his drama. In some old sketch book, possibly even in some old print, he may yet find some convincing evidence that he is right. But the Ilbridge House of today is not that

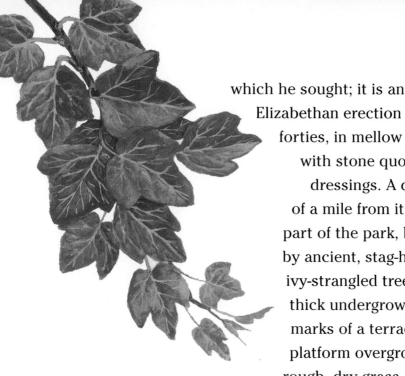

which he sought; it is an
Elizabethan erection of the
forties, in mellow red brick,
with stone quoins and
dressings. A quarter
of a mile from it, in a low
part of the park, backed
by ancient, stag-horned,
ivy-strangled trees and
thick undergrowth, are
marks of a terraced
platform overgrown with
rough, dry grass. A few
stone balusters lie here and there, and a heap or two, covered
with nettles, brambles, and ivy, of wrought stones with badly
carved crockets. This, someone told Mr. Dillet, was the site
of a much older house. As he
drove out of the village,
the hall clock
suddenly struck
four and Mr. Dillet
started up and
clapped his hands
over his ears as if he
had been struck. It was
not the first time he had
heard that bell.

84

Awaiting an offer from the other side of the Atlantic, the dolls' house still reposes, carefully sheeted, in a loft over Mr. Dillet's stables, whither Collins conveyed it on the day when Mr. Dillet started for the sea coast.

A CHRISTMAS CAROL

Charles Dickens
Extract

Scrooge took his melancholy dinner in his usual melancholy tavern; and having read all the newspapers, and beguiled the rest of the evening with his banker's book, went home to bed. He lived in chambers which had once belonged to his deceased partner. They were a gloomy suite of rooms, in a lowering pile of building up a yard, where it had so little business to be, that one could scarcely help fancying it must have run there when it was a young house, playing at hide-and-seek with other houses, and have forgotten the way out again. It was old enough now, and dreary enough, for nobody lived in it but Scrooge, the other rooms being all let out as offices. The yard was so dark that even Scrooge, who knew its every stone, was fain to grope with his hands. The fog and frost so hung about the black old gateway of the house, that it seemed as if the Genius of the Weather sat in mournful meditation on the threshold.

Now, it is a fact, that there was nothing at all particular about the knocker on the door, except that it was very large. It is also a fact, that Scrooge had seen it, night and morning, during his whole residence in that place; also that Scrooge had as little of what is called fancy about him as any man in the City of London, even including – which is a bold word – the corporation, aldermen, and livery. Let it also be borne in mind that Scrooge had not bestowed one thought on Marley since his last mention of his seven-years dead partner that afternoon. And then let any man explain to me, if he can, how it happened that Scrooge, having his key in the lock of the door, saw in the knocker, without its undergoing any intermediate process of change: not a knocker, but Marley's face.

Marley's face. It was not in impenetrable shadow as the other objects in the yard were, but had a dismal light about it, like a bad lobster in a dark cellar. It was not angry or ferocious, but looked at Scrooge as Marley used to look: with ghostly spectacles turned up

upon its ghostly forehead. The hair was curiously stirred, as if by breath or hot air; and, though the eyes were wide open, they were perfectly motionless. That, and its livid color, made it horrible; but its horror seemed to be in spite of the face and beyond its control, rather than a part of its own expression.

As Scrooge looked fixedly at this phenomenon, it was a knocker again.

To say that he was not startled, or that his blood was not conscious of a terrible sensation to which it had been a stranger from infancy, would be untrue. But he put his hand upon the key he had relinquished, turned it sturdily, walked in, and lit his candle.

He *did* pause, with a moment's irresolution, before he shut the door; and he *did* look cautiously behind it first, as if he half expected to be terrified with the sight of Marley's pigtail sticking out into the hall. But there was nothing on the back of the door, except the screws and nuts that held the knocker on, so he said "Pooh, pooh!" and closed it with a bang.

The sound resounded through the house like thunder. Every room above, and every cask in the wine merchant's cellars below, appeared to have a separate peal of echoes of its own. Scrooge was not a man to be frightened by echoes. He fastened the door, and walked across the hall, and up the stairs, slowly too, trimming his candle as he went.

You may talk vaguely about driving a coach-and-six up a good old flight of stairs, or through a bad young Act of Parliament; but I mean to say you might have got a hearse up that staircase – and taken it broadwise, with the splinter bar toward the wall and the door toward the balustrades – and done it easy. There was plenty of width for that, and room to spare; which is perhaps the reason why Scrooge thought he saw a locomotive hearse going on before him in the gloom. Half-a-dozen gas lamps out of the street wouldn't have lit the entry too well, so you may suppose that it was pretty dark with Scrooge's dip.

Up Scrooge went, not caring a button for that: darkness is cheap, and Scrooge liked it. But before he shut his heavy door, he walked through his rooms to see that all was right. He had just enough recollection of the face to desire to do that.

Sitting room, bedroom, lumber room. All as they should be. Nobody under the table, nobody under the sofa; a small fire in the grate; spoon and basin ready; and the little saucepan of gruel (Scrooge had a cold in his head) upon the hob. Nobody under the bed; nobody in the closet; nobody in his dressing gown, which was hanging up in a suspicious attitude against the wall. Lumber room as usual. Old fire guard, old shoes, two fish baskets, wash stand on three legs, and a poker.

Quite satisfied, he closed his door, and locked himself in; double locked himself in, which was not his custom. Thus secured against surprise, he took off his cravat; put on his dressing gown and slippers, and his night cap; and sat down before the fire to take his gruel.

It was a very low fire indeed; nothing on such a bitter night. He was obliged to sit close to it and brood over it before he could extract the least sensation of warmth from such a handful of fuel. The fireplace was an old one, built by some Dutch merchant long ago, and paved all round with quaint Dutch tiles, designed to illustrate the Scriptures. There were Cains and Abels, Pharaoh's daughters, Queens of Sheba, Angelic messengers descending through the air on clouds like feather beds, Abrahams, Belshazzars, Apostles putting off to sea in butter boats, hundreds of figures to attract his thoughts; and yet that face of Marley, seven years dead, came like the ancient Prophet's rod, and swallowed up the whole. If each smooth tile had been a blank at first, with power to shape some picture on its surface from the disjointed fragments of his thoughts, there would have been a copy of old Marley's head on every one.

"Humbug!" said Scrooge; and walked across the room.

After several turns, he sat down again. As he threw his head back in the chair, his glance happened to rest upon a bell, a disused bell, that hung in the room, and communicated for some purpose now forgotten with a chamber in the highest story of the building. It was with great astonishment, and with a strange, inexplicable dread, that as he looked, he saw this bell begin to swing. It swung so softly in the outset that it scarcely made a sound; but soon it rang out loudly, and so did every bell in the house.

This might have lasted half a minute, or a minute, but it seemed an hour. The bells ceased as they had begun, together. They were succeeded by a clanking noise, deep down below; as if some person were dragging a heavy chain over the casks in the wine merchant's cellar. Scrooge then remembered to have heard that ghosts in haunted houses were described as dragging chains.

The cellar door flew open with a booming sound, and then he heard the noise much louder, on the floors below; then coming up the stairs; then coming straight toward his door.

"It's humbug still!" said Scrooge. "I won't believe it."

His color changed though, when, without a pause, it came on through the heavy door, and passed into the room before his eyes. Upon its coming in, the dying flame leaped up, as though it cried, "I know him! Marley's Ghost!" and fell again.

The same face: the very same. Marley in his pigtail, usual waistcoat, tights and boots; the tassels on the latter bristling like his pigtail, and his coat skirts, and the hair upon his head. The chain he drew was clasped about his middle. It was long, and wound about him like a tail; and it was made (for Scrooge observed it closely) of cash boxes, keys, padlocks, ledgers, deeds, and heavy purses wrought in steel. His body was transparent: so that Scrooge, observing him, and looking through his waistcoat, could see the two buttons on his coat behind.

Scrooge had often heard it said that Marley had no bowels, but he had never believed it until now.

No, nor did he believe it even now. Though he looked the phantom through and through, and saw it standing before him; though he felt the chilling influence of its death-cold

eyes; and marked the very texture of the folded kerchief bound about its head and chin, which wrapper he had not observed before; he was still incredulous, and fought against his senses.

"How now," said Scrooge, caustic and cold as ever. "What do you want with me?"

"Much." It was Marley's voice, no doubt about it.

"Who are you?"

"Ask me who I was."

"Who were you then?" said Scrooge, raising his voice. "You're particular – for a shade." He was going to say "to a shade," but substituted this as more appropriate.

"In life I was your business partner, Jacob Marley."

"Can you – can you sit down?" asked Scrooge, looking doubtfully at him.

"I can."

"Do it, then."

Scrooge asked the question because he didn't know whether a ghost so transparent might find himself in a condition to take a chair, and felt that in the event of its being impossible, it might involve the necessity of an embarrassing explanation. But the ghost sat down on the opposite side of the fireplace, as if he were quite used to it.

"You don't believe in me," observed the Ghost.

"I don't," said Scrooge.

"What evidence would you have of my reality beyond that of your senses?"

"I don't know," said Scrooge.

"Why do you doubt your senses?"

"Because," said Scrooge, "a little thing affects them. A slight disorder of the stomach makes them cheats. You may be an undigested bit of beef, a blot of mustard, a crumb of cheese, a fragment of an underdone potato. There's more of gravy than of grave about you, whatever you are!"

Scrooge was not much in the habit of cracking jokes, nor did he feel, in his heart, by any means waggish then. The truth is that he tried to be smart as a means of distracting his own attention, and keeping down his terror; for the spectre's voice disturbed the very marrow in his bones.

To sit, staring at those fixed, glazed eyes in silence for a moment, would play, Scrooge felt, the very deuce with him. There was something very awful, too, in the specter's being provided with an infernal atmosphere of its own. Scrooge could not feel it himself, but this was clearly the case; for though the Ghost sat perfectly motionless, its hair, and skirts, and tassels, were still agitated as by the hot vapor from an oven.

"You see this toothpick?" said Scrooge, returning quickly to the charge, for the reason just assigned; and wishing, though it were only for a second, to divert the vision's stony gaze from himself.

"I do," replied the Ghost.

"You are not looking at it," said Scrooge.

"But I see it," said the Ghost, "notwithstanding."

"Well," returned Scrooge, "I have but to swallow this, and be for the rest of my days persecuted by a legion of goblins, all of my own creation. Humbug, I tell you: humbug!"

At this the spirit raised a frightful cry, and shook its chain with such a dismal and appalling noise that Scrooge held on tight to his chair, to save himself from falling in a swoon. But how much greater was his horror when the phantom, taking off the bandage round its head as if it were too warm to wear in-doors, its lower jaw dropped down upon its breast!

Scrooge fell upon his knees, and clasped his hands before his face.

"Mercy!" he said. "Dreadful apparition, why do you trouble me?"

"Man of the worldly mind!" replied the Ghost. "Do you believe in me or not?"

"I do," said Scrooge. "I must. But why do spirits walk the earth, and why do they come to me?"

"It is required of every man," the Ghost returned, "that the spirit within him should walk abroad among his fellow-men, and travel far and wide; and if that spirit goes not forth in life, it is condemned to do so after death. It is doomed to wander through the world – oh, woe is me! – and witness what it cannot share, but might have shared on earth, and turned to happiness."

Again the specter raised a cry, and shook its chain and wrung its shadowy hands.

"You are fettered," said Scrooge, trembling. "Tell me why?"

"I wear the chain I forged in life," replied the Ghost. "I made it link by link, and yard by yard; I girded it on of my own free will, and of my own free will I wore it. Is its pattern strange to you?"

Scrooge trembled more and more.

"Or would you know," pursued the Ghost, "the weight and length of the strong coil you bear yourself? It was full as heavy and as long as this, seven Christmas Eves ago. You have labored on it, since. It is a ponderous chain!"

Scrooge glanced about him on the floor, in the expectation of finding himself surrounded by some fifty or sixty fathoms of iron cable, but he could see nothing.

"Jacob," he said, imploringly. "Old Jacob Marley, tell me more. Speak comfort to me, Jacob."

"I have none to give," the Ghost replied. "It comes from other regions, Ebenezer Scrooge, and is conveyed by other ministers, to other kinds of men. Nor can I tell you what I would. A very little more is all permitted to me. I cannot rest, I cannot stay, I cannot linger anywhere. My spirit never walked beyond our countinghouse – mark me! – in life my spirit never roved beyond the narrow limits of our money-changing hole; and weary journeys lie before me!"

It was a habit with Scrooge, whenever he became thoughtful, to put his hands in his breeches pockets. Pondering on what the Ghost had said, he did so now, but without lifting up his eyes or getting off his knees.

"You must have been very slow about it, Jacob," Scrooge observed, in a businesslike manner, though with humility and deference.

"Slow!" the Ghost repeated.

"Seven years dead," mused Scrooge. "And traveling all the time?"

"The whole time," said the Ghost. "No rest, no peace. Incessant torture of remorse."

"You travel fast?" said Scrooge.

"On the wings of the wind," replied the Ghost.

"You might have got over a great quantity of ground in seven years," said Scrooge.

The Ghost, on hearing this, set up another cry, and clanked its chain so hideously in the dead silence of the night, that the Ward would have been justified in indicting it for a nuisance.

"Oh! Captive, bound, and double ironed," cried the phantom, "not to know, that ages of incessant labor by immortal creatures, for this earth must pass into eternity before the good of which it is susceptible is all developed! Not to know that any Christian spirit working kindly in its little sphere, whatever it may be, will find its mortal life too short for its vast means of usefulness! Not to know that no space of regret can make amends for one life's opportunity misused! Yet such was I! Oh! such was I!"

"But you were always a good man of business, Jacob," faltered Scrooge, who now began to apply this to himself.

"Business!" cried the Ghost, wringing its hands again. "Mankind was my business. The common welfare was my business; charity, mercy, forbearance, and benevolence were all my business. The dealings of my trade were but a drop of water in the comprehensive ocean of my business!"

It held up its chain at arm's length, as if that were the cause of all its unavailing grief, and flung it heavily upon the ground again.

"At this time of the rolling year," the specter said, "I suffer most. Why did I walk through crowds of fellow-beings with my eyes turned down, and never raise them to that blessed Star which led the Wise Men to a poor abode? Were there no poor homes to which its light would have conducted me?"

Scrooge was very much dismayed to hear the specter going on at this rate, and began to quake exceedingly.

"Hear me!" cried the Ghost. "My time is nearly gone."

"I will," said Scrooge. "But don't be hard upon me. Don't be flowery, Jacob! Pray!"

"How it is that I appear before you in a shape that you can see, I may not tell. I have sat invisible beside you many and many a day."

It was not an agreeable idea. Scrooge shivered, and wiped the perspiration from his brow.

"That is no light part of my penance," pursued the Ghost. "I am here tonight to warn you, that you have yet a chance and hope of escaping my fate. A chance and hope of my procuring, Ebenezer."

"You were always a good friend to me," said Scrooge. "Thank'ee."

"You will be haunted," resumed the Ghost, "by Three Spirits."

Scrooge's countenance fell almost as low as the Ghost's had done.

"Is that the chance and hope you mentioned, Jacob?" he demanded, in a faltering voice.

"It is."

"I-I think I'd rather not," said Scrooge.

"Without their visits," said the Ghost, "you cannot hope to shun the path I tread. Expect the first tomorrow, when the bell tolls one."

"Couldn't I take them all at once, and have it over, Jacob?" hinted Scrooge.

"Expect the second on the next night at the same hour. The third upon the next night when the last stroke of twelve has ceased to vibrate. Look to see me no more; and look that, for your own sake, you remember what has passed between us!"

When it had said these words, the specter took its wrapper from the table, and bound it round its head, as before. Scrooge knew this, by the smart sound its teeth made, when the jaws were brought together by the bandage. He ventured to raise his eyes again, and found his supernatural visitor confronting him in an erect attitude, with its chain wound over and about its arm.

The apparition walked backward from him; and at every step it took, the window raised itself a little, so that when the specter reached it, it was wide open.

It beckoned Scrooge to approach, which he did. When they were within two paces of each other, Marley's Ghost held up its hand, warning him to come no nearer. Scrooge stopped.

Not so much in obedience, as in surprise and fear: for on the raising of the hand, he became sensible of confused noises in the air; incoherent sounds of lamentation and regret; wailings inexpressibly sorrowful and self-accusatory. The specter, after listening for a moment, joined in the mournful dirge; and floated out upon the bleak, dark night.

Scrooge followed to the window, desperate in his curiosity. He looked out.

The air was filled with phantoms, wandering hither and thither in restless haste, and moaning as they went. Everyone of them wore chains like Marley's Ghost, some few (they might be guilty governments) were linked together, none were free.

Many had been personally known to Scrooge in their lives. He had been quite familiar with one old ghost, in a white waistcoat, with a monstrous iron safe attached to its ankle, who cried piteously at being unable to assist a wretched woman with an infant, whom it saw below, upon a doorstep. The misery with them all was, clearly, that they sought to interfere, for good, in human matters, and had lost the power forever.

Whether these creatures faded into mist, or mist enshrouded them, he could not tell. But they and their spirit voices faded together, and the night became as it had been when he walked home.

Scrooge closed the window, and examined the door by which the Ghost had entered. It was double locked, as he had locked it with his own hands, and the bolts were undisturbed. He tried to say "Humbug!" but stopped at the first syllable. And being, from the emotion he had undergone, or the fatigues of the day, or his glimpse of the "invisible world," or the dull conversation of the Ghost, or the lateness of the hour, much in need of repose; went straight to bed, without undressing, and fell asleep upon the instant.

THE SHIP THAT SAW A GHOST

Frank Norris
Extract

So the *Glarus* plodded and churned her way onward. Every day and all day the same pale blue sky and unwinking sun bent over that moving speck. Every day and all day the same black-blue water world, untouched by any known wind, smooth as a slab of syenite, colorful as an opal, stretched out and around and beyond and before and behind us, forever, illimitable, empty. Every day, the smoke of our fires veiled the streaked whiteness of our wake. Every day Hardenberg (our skipper) at noon pricked a pin hole in the chart that hung in the wheel house, and that showed we were so much farther into the wilderness. Every day the world of

102

men, of civilization, of newspapers, policemen, and street railways, receded, and we steamed on alone, lost and forgotten in that silent sea.

"Jolly lot o' room to turn raound in," observed Ally Bazan, the colonial, "withaout steppin' on y'r neighbor's toes."

"We're clean, clean out o' the track of navigation," Hardenberg told him. "An' a blessed good thing for us, too. Nobody ever comes down into these waters. Ye couldn't pick no course here. Everything leads to nowhere."

"Might as well be in a bally balloon," said Strokher.

I shall not tell of the nature of the venture on which the *Glarus* was bound, further than to say it was not legitimate. It had to do with an ill thing done more than two centuries ago. There was money in the venture, but it was to be gained by a violation of metes and bounds which are better left intact.

The island toward which we were heading is associated in the minds of men with a horror. A ship had called there once, two hundred years in advance of the *Glarus* – a ship not much unlike the crank high-prowed caravel of Hudson – and her company had landed, and having accomplished the evil they had set out to do, made shift to sail away. And then, just after the palms of the island had sunk from sight below the water's edge, the unspeakable had happened. The death that was not death had arisen from out the sea and stood before the ship, and over it and the blight of the thing lay along the decks like mold, and the ship sweated in the terror of that which is yet without a name. Twenty men died in the first week, all but six in the second. These six, with the shadow of insanity upon them, made out to launch a boat, returned to the island and died there, after leaving a record of what had happened.

The six left the ship exactly as she was, sails all set, lanterns all lit – left her in the shadow of the death that was not death. The wind made at the time, they said, and as they bent to their bars, she sailed after them for all the world like a thing refusing to abandon them or be herself abandoned, till the wind died down. Then they left her behind, and she stood there, becalmed, and watched them go. She was never heard of again.

Or was she – well, that's as may be.

But the main point of the whole affair, to my notion, has always been this. The ship was the last friend of those six poor wretches who made back for the island with their poor chests of plunder. She was their guardian, as it were, would have defended and befriended them to the last; and also we, the Three Black Crows and myself, had no right under heaven, nor before the law of men, to come prying and peeping into this business – into this affair of the dead and buried past. There was sacrilege in it. We were no better than body snatchers.

When I heard the others complaining of the loneliness of our surroundings, I said nothing at first. I was no sailor man and I was on board only by tolerance. But I looked again at the maddening sameness of the horizon – the same vacant, void horizon that we had seen now for sixteen days on end, and felt in my wits and in my nerves that same formless rebellion and protest such as comes when the same note is reiterated over and over again.

It may seem a little thing that the mere fact of meeting with no other ship should have ground down the edge of the spirit. But let the incredulous – bound upon such a hazard as ours – sail straight into nothingness for sixteen days on end, seeing nothing but the sun, hearing nothing but the thresh of his own screw, and then put the question.

And yet, of all things, we desired no company. Stealth was our one great aim. But I think there were moments – towards the last – when the Three Crows would have welcomed even a cruiser.

On the seventh day, Hardenberg and I were forward by the cathead, adjusting the grain with some half-formed intent of spearing the porpoises that of late had begun to appear under our bows, and Hardenberg had been computing the number of days we were yet to run.

"We are some five hundred odd miles off that island by now," he said, "and she's doing her thirteen knots handsome. All's well so far – but do you know, I'd just as soon raise that point o' land as soon as convenient."

"How so?" said I, bending on the line. "Expect some weather?"

"Mr. Dixon," said he, giving me a curious glance, "the sea is a queer proposition, put it any ways. I've been a sea-farin' man since I was as big as a minute, and I know the sea, and what's more, the Feel o' the Sea. Now, look out yonder. Nothin', hey? Nothin' but the same ol' skyline we've watched all the way out. The glass is as steady as a steeple, and this ol' hooker, I reckon, is as sound as the day she went off the ways. But just the same, if I were to home now, a-foolin' about

Gloucester way in my little dough-dish – d'ye know what? I'd put into port. I sure would. Because why? Because I got the Feel o' the Sea, Mr. Dixon. I got the Feel o' the Sea."

I had heard old skippers say something of this before, and I cited to Hardenberg the experience of a skipper captain I once knew who had turned turtle in a calm sea off Trincomalee. I asked what this Feel of the Sea was warning him against just now (for on the high sea any premonition is a premonition of evil, not of good). But he was not explicit.

"I don't know," he answered moodily, and as if in great perplexity, coiling the rope as he spoke. "I don't know. There's some blame thing or other close to us, I'll bet a hat. I don't know the name of it, Mr. Dixon, and I don't know the game of it, but there's a big bird in the air, just out of sight someres, and," he suddenly exclaimed, smacking his knee and leaning forward, "I – don't – like – it – one – dam' – bit."

The same thing came up in our talk in the cabin that night, after the dinner was taken off, and we settled down to tobacco. Only, at this time, Hardenberg was on duty on the bridge. It was Ally Bazan who spoke instead.

"Seems to me," he hazarded, "as haow they's somethin' or other a-goin' to bump up, pretty blyme soon. I shouldn't be surprised, naow, y'know, if we piled her up on some bally uncharted reef along o' tonight and went strite daown afore we'd had a bloomin' charnce to s'y 'So long, gen'lemen all.'"

He laughed as he spoke, but when, just at that moment, a pan clattered in the galley, he jumped suddenly with an oath, and looked hard about the cabin.

106

Then Strokher confessed to a sense of distress also. He'd been having it since day before yesterday, it seemed.

"And I put it to you the glass is lovely," he said, "so it's no blow. I guess," he continued, "we're all a bit seedy and ship sore."

And whether or not this talk worked upon my own nerves, or whether in very truth the feel of the sea had found me also, I do not know; but I do know that after dinner that night, just before going to bed, a queer sense of apprehension came upon me, and that when I had come to my stateroom, I became furiously angry with nobody in particular, because I could not at once find the matches. But here was a difference. The other men had been merely vaguely uncomfortable.

I could put a name to my uneasiness. I felt that we were being watched.

It was a strange ship's company we made after that. I speak only of the Crows and myself. We carried a scant crew of stokers, and there was also a chief engineer. But we saw so little of him that he did not count. The Crows and I gloomed on the quarter deck from dawn to dark: silent, irritable, working upon each other's nerves till the creak of a block would make a man jump like cold steel laid to his flesh. We quarreled over nothing, glowered at each other for half a word, and each one of us, at different times, was at some pains to declare that never in the course of his career had he been associated with such a disagreeable trio of brutes. Yet we were always together and sought each other's company.

Only once were we all agreed, and that was when the cook, a Chinaman, spoiled a certain batch of biscuits. Unanimously we fell foul of the creature with so much vociferation as fishwives till he fled the cabin in actual fear of mishandling, leaving us suddenly seized with noisy hilarity – for the first time in a week. Hardenberg proposed a round of drinks from our single remaining case of beer. We stood up and formed an Elk's chain and then drained our glasses to each other's health.

That same evening, I remember, we all sat on the quarterdeck till late and – oddly enough – related each one his life's history up to date; and then went down to the cabin for a game of euchre before turning in.

We had left Strokher on the bridge – it was his watch – and had forgotten all about him in the interest of the game, when – I suppose it was about one in the morning – I heard him whistle long and shrill. I laid down my cards and said, "Hark!"

In the silence that followed we heard at first only the muffled lope of our engines, the cadenced snorting of the exhaust, and the ticking of Hardenberg's big watch in his waistcoat. Then from the bridge, above our deck, prolonged, intoned – a wailing cry in the night – came Strokher's voice: "Sail oh-h-h."

And the cards fell from our hands, and, like men turned to stone, we sat looking at each other across the soiled red cloth for what seemed an immeasurably long minute. Then stumbling and swearing, in a hysteria of hurry, we gained the deck.

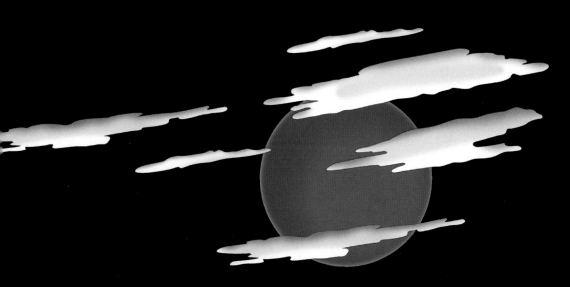

There was a moon, very low and reddish, but no wind. The sea beyond the taffrail was as smooth as lava, and so still that the swells from the cutwater of the *Glarus* did not break as they rolled away from the bows.

I remember that I stood staring and blinking at the empty ocean – where the moonlight lay like a painted stripe reaching to the horizon – stupid and frowning, till Hardenberg, who had gone on ahead, cried, "Not here – on the bridge!"

We joined Strokher, and as I came up the others were asking, "Where? Where?"

And there, before he had pointed, I saw – we all of us saw. And I heard Hardenberg's teeth come together like a spring trap, while Ally Bazan ducked as though to a blow, muttering, "Gord'a mercy, what nyme do ye put to a ship like that?"

And after that no one spoke for a long minute, and we stood there, moveless black shadows, huddled together for the sake of the blessed elbow touch that means so incalculably much, looking off over our port quarter.

For the ship that we saw there – oh, she was not a half-mile distant – was unlike any ship known to present day construction.

She was short, and high-pooped, and her stern, which was turned a little toward us, we could see, was set with curious windows, not unlike a house. And on either side of this stern were two great iron cressets such as once were used to burn signal fires in. She had three masts with mighty yards swung 'thwart ship, but bare of all sails save a few rotting streamers. Here and there about her a tangled mass of rigging drooped and sagged.

And there she lay, in the red eye of the setting moon, in that solitary ocean, shadowy, antique, forlorn, a thing the most abandoned, the most sinister I ever remember to have seen.

Then Strokher began to explain volubly and with many repetitions.

"A derelict, of course. I was asleep; yes I was asleep. Gross neglect of duty. And we worked up to her. When I woke, why – you see, when I woke, there she was," he gave a weak little laugh, "and – and now, why, there she is, you see. I turned around and saw her sudden like – when I woke up, that is."

He laughed again, and as he laughed, the engines far below our feet gave a sudden hiccup. Something crashed and struck the ship's sides till we lurched as we stood. There was a shriek of steam, a shout – and then silence.

The noise of the machinery ceased; the *Glarus* slid through the still water, moving only by her own decreasing momentum.

Hardenberg sang, "Stand by!" and called down the tube to the engine room.

"What's up?"

I was standing close enough to him to hear the answer in a small faint voice:

"Shaft gone, sir."

"Broke?"

"Yes, sir."

Hardenberg faced about. "Come below. We must talk."

I do not think any of us cast a glance at the other ship again. Certainly I kept my eyes away from her. But as we started down the companionway, I laid my hand on Strokher's shoulder. I looked him straight between the eyes as I asked, "*Were* you asleep? Is that why you saw her so suddenly?"

It is now five years since I asked the question. I am still waiting for Strokher's answer.

Well, our shaft was broken. We went down into the engine room and saw the jagged fracture that was the symbol of our broken hopes. And in the course of the next five minutes' conversation with the chief, we found that there was to be no mending of it. We said nothing about the mishap coinciding with the appearance of the ship. But I know we did not consider the break with any degree of surprise after a few moments.

We came slowly up from the engine room and sat down at the cabin table in a dispirited fashion.

"Now what?" said Hardenberg, by way of beginning.

Nobody answered at first.

It was by now three in the morning. I recall it all perfectly. The ports opposite where I sat were open and I could see. The moon was all but full set. The dawn was coming up with a copper murkiness over the edge of the world. All the stars were yet out. The sea, for all the red moon and copper dawn, was gray, and there, less than half a mile away, still lay our consort. I could see her through the portholes with each slow careening of the *Glarus*.

"I vote for the island," cried Ally Bazan, "shaft or no shaft. We rigs a bit o' syle, y'know," – and thereat the discussion began.

For upwards of two hours it raged, with loud words and shaken forefingers, and great noisy bangings of the table, and how it would have ended I do not know, but at last – it was then maybe five in the morning – the lookout passed word down to the cabin, "Will you come on deck, gentlemen?" It was the mate who spoke, and the man was shaken – I could see that – to the very vitals of him.

We stared at one another, and I watched little Ally Bazan go slowly white to the lips. And even then no word of the Ship, except as it might be this from Hardenberg, "What is it? Good God Almighty, I'm no coward, but this thing is getting one too many for me." Then without further speech he went on deck.

The air was cool. The sun was not yet up. It was that strange, queer, mid-period between dark and dawn, when the night is over and the day not yet come, just the gray that is neither light nor dark, the dim dead blink as of the refracted light from extinct worlds.

We stood at the rail. We did not speak; we stood watching. It was so still that the drip of steam from some loosened pipe far below was plainly audible, and it sounded in that lifeless, silent grayness, like – God knows what – a death tick.

"You see," said the mate, speaking just above a whisper, "there's no mistake about it. She is moving – this way."

"Oh, a current, of course," Strokher tried to say cheerfully, "sets her toward us."

Would the morning never come?

Ally Bazan – his parents were Catholic – began to mutter to himself.

Then Hardenberg spoke aloud.

"I particularly don't want – that – out – there – to cross our bows. I don't want it to come to that. We must get some sails on her."

"And I put it to you as man to man," said Strokher, "where might be your wind?"

He was right. The *Glarus* floated in absolute calm. On all that slab of ocean, nothing moved but the dead ship.

She came on slowly; her bows, the high clumsy bows pointed toward us, the water turning from her forefoot. She came on; she was near at hand. We saw her plainly – saw the rotted planks, the crumbling rigging, the rust-corroded metalwork, the broken rail, the gaping deck – and I could imagine that the clean water broke away from her sides in refluent wavelets as though in recoil from a thing unclean. She made no sound. No single thing stirred aboard the hulk of her – but she moved.

We were helpless. The *Glarus* could stir no boat in any direction; we were chained to the spot. Nobody had thought to put out our lights, and they still burned on through the dawn, strangely out of place in their red and green garishness.

And in the silence of that empty ocean, in that queer half-light between dawn and day, at six o'clock, silent as the settling of the dead to the bottomless bottom of the ocean, gray as fog, lonely, blind, soulless, voiceless, the dead ship crossed our bows.

I do not know how long after this the ship disappeared, or what was the time of day when we at last pulled ourselves together. But we came to some sort of decision at last. This was to go on – under sail. We were too close to the island now to turn back for – for a broken shaft.

The afternoon was spent fitting on the sails to her, and when after nightfall the wind at length came up fresh and favorable, I believe we all felt heartened and a deal more hardy – until the last canvass went aloft, and Hardenberg took the wheel.

We had drifted a good deal since the morning, and the bows of the *Glarus* were pointed homeward, but as soon as the breeze blew strong enough to get steerage way, Hardenberg put the wheel over, and headed for the island again.

We had not gone on this course half an hour – no, not twenty minutes – before the wind shifted a whole quarter of the compass and took the *Glarus* square in the teeth, so that there was nothing for it but to tack. And then the strangest thing befell.

I will make allowance for the fact that there was no center board nor keel to speak of to the *Glarus*. I will admit that the sails upon a 900-ton freighter are not calculated to speed her, nor steady her. I will even admit the possibility of a current that set from the island toward us. All this may be true, yet the *Glarus* should have advanced. We should have made a wake.

Instead of this, our stolid, steady, trusty old boat was – what shall I say?

I will say that no man may thoroughly understand a ship – after all. I will say that new ships are cranky and unsteady, that old and seasoned ships have their little crotchets, their little fussinesses that their skippers must learn and humor if they are to get anything out of them; that even the best ships may sulk at times, shirk their work, grow unstable, perverse, and refuse to answer helm and handling. And I will say that some ships that for years have sailed blue water as soberly and as docilely as a streetcar horse has plodded the treadmill of the 'tween-tracks, have been known to balk, as stubbornly and as conclusively as any old Bay Billy that ever wore a bell. I know this has happened, because I have seen it. I saw, for instance, the *Glarus* do it.

Quite literally and truly we could do nothing with her. We will say, if you like, that that great jar and wrench when the shaft gave way shook her and crippled her. It is true, however, that whatever the cause may have been, we could not force her toward the island. Of course, we all said "current;" but why didn't the logline trail?

For three days and three nights we tried it. And the *Glarus* heaved and plunged and shook herself just as you have seen a horse plunge and rear when his rider tries to force him at the steamroller.

I tell you I could feel the fabric of her tremble and shudder from bow to stern post, as though she were in a storm; I tell you she fell off from the wind, and broad-on drifted back from her course till the sensation of her shrinking was as plain as her own staring lights and a thing pitiful to see.

We rowelled her and we crowded sail upon her, and we coaxed and bullied and humored her, till the Three Crows, their fortune only a plain sail two days ahead, raved and swore like insensate brutes, or shall we say like *mahouts*, trying to drive their stricken elephant upon the tiger – and all to no purpose. "Damn the damned current and the damned luck and the damned shaft and all," Hardenberg would exclaim, as from the wheel he would watch the *Glarus* falling off. "Go on, you old hooker – you tub of junk! My God, you'd think she was scared!"

Perhaps the *Glarus* was scared; that point is debatable. But it was beyond doubt or debate that Hardenberg was scared.

A ship that will not obey is only one degree less terrible than a mutinous crew. And we were in a fair way to have both. The stokers whom we had impressed into duty as A.B.'s, were of course superstitious. They had seen – what we had seen and they knew how the *Glarus* was acting and it was only a question of time before they got out of hand.

That was the end. We held a final conference in the cabin and decided that there was no help for it – we must turn back.

And back we accordingly turned, and at once the wind followed us, and the "current" helped us, and the water churned under the forefoot of the *Glarus*, and the wake whitened under her stern, and the logline ran out from the rail and strained back as the ship worked homeward.

We had never a mishap from the time we finally swung her about; and, considering the circumstances, the voyage back to San Francisco was propitious.

But an incident happened just after we had started back. We were perhaps some five miles on the homeward track. It was early evening and Strokher had the watch. At about seven o'clock he called me up on the bridge. "See her?" he said.

And there, far behind us, in the shadow of the twilight, loomed the other ship again, desolate, lonely beyond words. We were leaving her rapidly astern. Strokher and I stood looking at her till she dwindled to a dot. Then Strokher said: "She's on post again."

And when months afterward we limped into the Golden Gate and cast anchor off the front, our crew went ashore as soon as discharged, and in half a dozen hours the legend was in every sailors' boarding house and in every seaman's dive, from Barbary Coast to Black Tom's.

It is still there; and that is why no pilot will take the *Glarus* out, no captain will navigate her, no stoker feed her fires, no sailor walk her decks. The *Glarus* is suspect. She will never smell blue water again. She has seen a ghost.

Emily Brontë
1818 – 1848
England

The classic tale *Wuthering Heights* (1847) is set on the wild, bleak Yorkshire moors that surrounded Emily Brontë's home in England. Although Brontë wrote only one novel, scholars consider *Wuthering Heights* the most intense novel written in the English language.

Emily Brontë was born in Thornton, Yorkshire. Her father was a rector, and her mother died when Emily was just three years old. Emily spent most of her childhood reading and composing stories with her sisters Anne and Charlotte and their brother Branwell. Charlotte, Emily, and Anne, published a volume of verse under the pseudonyms Currer, Ellis, and Acton Bell.

Although *Wuthering Heights* did not achieve the popular success of Charlotte's *Jane Eyre* at the time, today it is considered a masterpiece. *Wuthering Heights* is told in a series of flashbacks and time shifts, and some scholars think her style of narration may have influenced Mary Shelley's *Frankenstein*.

Emily's brother Branwell died in 1848. Emily became ill at his funeral and never recovered. She died of tuberculosis three months later, at the age of 30, just one year after the publication of her masterpiece. *Wuthering Heights*, however, lives on and has been translated to film several times.

Charles Dickens
1812 – 1870
England

Charles John Huffam Dickens was fascinated by the ghost stories his nurse read to him when he was young. His lifelong love of all things ghoulish and ghastly developed into a fascination with Spiritualism in his later life. As well as his world famous novels, Dickens wrote many supernatural stories – often published at Christmas time for festive storytelling fun. He is best known for his use of colorful characters and a focus on poor social and economic conditions.

Born in Hampshire, England, Charles Dickens was the second child of eight. His father was an eternal optimist who served as the prototype for the father of *Nicholas Nickleby* (1838-39) and Wilkins Micawber (*David Copperfield*, 1849-50).

Not one of Dickens's stories has ever gone out of print, and his writings have been made into more than 140 film versions. Among his most famous works are *Oliver Twist* (1837–39), *The Old Curiosity Shop* (1840–41), *A Christmas Carol* (1843), *David Copperfield* (1849–50), *Bleak House* (1852–53), *Hard Times* (1854), *A Tale of Two Cities* (1859), and *Great Expectations* (1860–61). He also created timeless characters, such as Ebenezer Scrooge and Miss Havisham, who have become legendary in their own right and practically live a life of their own in public imagination.

M. R. James
1862 – 1936
England (Kent)

Montague Rhodes James is best remembered for his horrifying tales of the supernatural, which often allude to creatures that are spidery, thin, hairy, and hooded or swathed in linen drapery. During his lifetime, James excelled as a medieval scholar who also catalogued libraries and studied biblical Apocrypha, church iconography, and folklore. He was drawn to local legends and traditional beliefs, which worked their way into his writings.

Born in Kent, England, James attended King's College in Cambridge. He wrote on a variety of academic subjects while working as an editor and translator of scholarly and literary works. His first collection, *Ghost Stories of an Antiquary*, was published in 1904. Several collections followed: *More Ghost Stories of an Antiquary* (1911), *A Thin Ghost and Others* (1919), *A Warning to the Curious and Other Ghost Stories* (1925), and *The Collected Ghost Stories of M.R. James* (1931). He also wrote a short supernatural fairytale novel for children, *The Five Jars* (1922).

During his time, it was popular to tell scary stories on Christmas Eve, and James's stories took prominence among them. They were particularly enjoyed because they usually pertained to a supernatural menace of something beyond the grave and contained the key elements of a classic ghost story.

J. Sheridan Le Fanu
1814 – 1873
Ireland

In his day, Joseph Thomas Sheridan Le Fanu was a bestselling author of works such as *Carmilla* (1871–1872) and *In a Glass Darkly* (1872). During the Victorian era, it was the custom, according to author Henry James, for hosts to place a volume of Le Fanu's stories on a guest's bedside table for "the hours after midnight." Although he is considered a forerunner of modern horror fiction and was widely read during his day, it remains a mystery that he is almost forgotten today.

The "father of the modern ghost story," Le Fanu was born in Dublin. In 1838, he published his first story, "The Ghost and the Bone-Setter." He later published the collections *Ghost Stories and Tales of Mystery* (1851) and *The Purcell Papers* (1880). His first novel was *The Clock and Anchor* (1845), and his best-known novel was the suspense story, *Uncle Silas* (1864).

Le Fanu's influence was far-reaching; his *Carmilla* served as inspiration for Bram Stoker's *Dracula*, and some scholars think *A Chapter in the History of the Tyrone Family* (1839) influenced Emily Brontë's *Wuthering Heights*. After his death, Le Fanu's work fell nearly into obscurity until ghost story writer M. R. James ("The Haunted Doll's House") published a collection of Le Fanu's stories under the title *Madam Crow's Ghost and Other Tales of Mystery* (1923).

Frank Norris
1870 – 1902
United States (Chicago, Illinois)

Benjamin Franklin Norris wrote meticulously researched novels during his short career. He was best known for his documentation of the effects of industry on agricultural communities. His ghost stories may be a product of his time as a reporter, when he conducted hundreds of interviews.

Born in Chicago, Illinois, Norris moved to San Francisco, California, where he met with other writers who assembled at the Bohemian Club. He studied philosophy at the University of California at Berkeley and transferred to Harvard College in 1895. There, he began work on one of his most memorable novels, *McTeague* (1899). Norris was a member of the Naturalist school of writers, who believed the lives of ordinary people were worthy of serious literary treatment. He also paid careful attention to authenticity and accurate details. He wrote a trilogy on San Francisco that included *McTeague*, *Blix* (1899), and *Vandover the Brute* (1914). He planned to write a second trilogy on the Epic of Wheat, and the drama of the industry, but only completed *The Octopus* (1901) and *The Pit* (1903).

He and his wife purchased a ranch from the widow of Robert Louis Stevenson ("The Body Snatcher"), but Norris's sudden death from appendicitis at the age of 32 prevented him from staying at the ranch for long.

Oscar Wilde
1854 – 1900
Ireland

Oscar Fingal O'Flahertie Wilde's life is nearly as fascinating to scholars as the lives of the characters he created. He was an Irish writer who composed poetry, plays, short stories, and just one novel, *The Picture of Dorian Gray* (1891). This supernatural tale so unsettled and shocked readers that it caused an uproar when it was first printed in *Lippincott's Magazine* in 1890. He remains a highly quoted literary figure for his witticisms.

Born in Dublin, Oscar Wilde was the son of a prominent surgeon and a well-known journalist. His mother held a regular Sunday afternoon discussion group which included J. Sheridan le Fanu (*Carmilla* and "The Narrative of the Ghost of a Hand").

Wilde became a notorious figure for his exaltation of the Aesthetic Movement, a philosophy that advocated "art for art's sake." He published essays, poems, two collections of children's stories, *The Happy Prince and Other Tales* (1888) and *The House of Pomegranates* (1892), and four wildly popular plays: *Lady Windermere's Fan* (1892), *A Woman of No Importance* (1893), *An Ideal Husband* (1895), and *The Importance of Being Earnest* (1895). Just a month before his death, Wilde is quoted as saying, "My wallpaper and I are fighting a duel to the death. One or the other of us has got to go."

GHASTLY GLOSSARY

apoplexy—stroke; sudden loss of consciousness

appellation—name

asseverated—affirmed or declared positively

bier—a framework for carrying a coffin

charnel house—a building in which bodies or bones are placed

clandestine—secret

confluence—a flowing together, meeting, or gathering at one point

countenance—the face, or the look or expression on the face, often revealing mood

efficacious—having the power to produce a desired effect

en secondes noces—French, meaning "in second weddings"

hooker—a single-masted fishing boat

importunate—urgent, overly persistent

in flagrante delicto—Latin, meaning, "while the crime is blazing" or in the act of committing indecency

lachrymose—tearful, mournful, given to tears

maxillary—pertaining to the jaw and teeth

obviate—to prevent or make unnecessary

ogival—arched

raiment—clothing, garments

sanguineous—of or relating to blood; blood red

sotto voce—Italian, meaning "under voice" or under the breath

veracious—truthful, honest

visage—face; appearance